After the Party: Reflections on Life since the CPGB

*In memory of Margot Heinemann,
Dave Cook and Monty Johnstone*

AFTER THE PARTY: REFLECTIONS ON LIFE SINCE THE CPGB

Edited by Andy Croft

London Lawrence & Wishart 2012

Lawrence and Wishart Limited
99a Wallis Road
London
E9 5LN

First published 2012

Collection © Lawrence & Wishart 2012
Individual articles (c) author

The authors have asserted their rights under the Copyright, Design and Patents Act, 1998 to be identified as the authors of this work.

All rights reserved. Apart from fair dealing for the purpose of private study, research, criticism or review, no part of this publication may be reproduced, stored in a retrieval system, or transmitted, in any form or by any means, electronic, electrical, chemical, mechanical, optical, photocopying, recording or otherwise, without the prior permission of the copyright owner.

British Library Cataloguing in Publication Data.
A catalogue record for this book is available from the British Library

ISBN 9781 907103 476

Text setting E-type, Liverpool

Contents

1. Introduction: It's my party and I'll cry if I want to 7
   Andy Croft

2. The revolution is just a T-shirt away 11
   Mark Perryman

3. A political error of vast proportions 33
   Kate Hudson

4. No future without Marx 49
   Alistair Findlay

5. Towards a marxist theory of love; *or* the personal is post-political 67
   Andrew Pearmain

6. We will rebuild our country ten times more beautiful 89
   Lorna Reith

7. The situation is still as it was 102
   Stuart Hill

8. The Party is dead, long live the party! 119
   Dave Cope

9. The democratisation of everything 138
   Andy Croft

   Notes on contributors 154
   Index 155

Introduction

It's my party and I'll cry if I want to

'The Party can never be obliterated,' wrote Brecht in *The Measures Taken*, 'for its methods are those of its philosophers / Which are based on the experience of reality / And are destined soon to transform it.' Unfortunately for this kind of teleology, historical events turned out rather differently, as twenty years ago communist parties everywhere found themselves transformed, and in many cases 'obliterated', by the experience of reality.

In November 1991, the Communist Party of Great Britain held its forty-third – and last – Congress at the TUC offices on Great Russell Street. Seventy-one years after the creation of the party in the revolutionary upsurge that followed the events of 1917, Congress delegates voted by a majority of two to one to replace the Party of Lenin with a loose and short-lived federal structure called Democratic Left. After the major political upheavals of the previous few months, the dissolution of the British Party was a barely noticed footnote to the larger story about the end of Communism in Europe.

It was a strangely muted end to a noisy and vociferous history. This was, after all, an organisation unlike any other in British politics. No other political party ever enjoyed so much influence in the trade union movement, or in British intellectual and cultural life. At its peak the party had 60,000 members, and during its life-time several hundred Communist councillors and five Members of Parliament were elected (including Britain's first Asian-born MP). It was even represented in the House of Lords. The *Daily Worker* once sold 120,000 copies a day. Notable party members (not always lifelong) included Sylvia Pankhurst, Henry Moore, Jimmy Reid, Doris Lessing, Claudia Jones, E.P. Thompson, Hugh McDiarmid, Tilda Swinton, Arnold

Wesker, J.D. Bernal, Sylvia Townsend Warner, Mick McGahey, Hamish Henderson and Beatrix Campbell. Many of the key moments in twentieth-century British history were unmistakably shaped by the contribution of the Communist Party – most obviously the General Strike, the Hunger Marches, the Battle of Cable Street, the formation of the International Brigades, the occupation of the London underground during the Blitz, the Forces parliaments, the Squatters Movement, the post-war dock strikes, the Edinburgh Festival Fringe, the Clydeside Apprentices Strike, the Notting Hill Carnival, the UCS work-in, Grunwick, the miners' strikes of 1971, 1974 and 1984 and the People's March for Jobs. Organisations like CND, the Anti-Apartheid Movement, the Movement for Colonial Freedom, and the Vietnam and Chile Solidarity Campaigns were maintained for many years by the hard work of individual party members.

By 1991, however, everybody knew that the party was over. Events elsewhere had made its continued existence untenable. Membership was down to less than 7,000. Most of its famous members had already left (or had been expelled). The party had long since lost control of the *Morning Star* (formerly the *Daily Worker*). A few weeks after the Congress, the party's influential magazine *Marxism Today* appeared on the news-stands for the last time with an apocalyptic front-cover announcing 'The End'.

In the two decades since then, the CP has been effectively airbrushed from the historical record. The party's achievements are now routinely credited to others. For example, the 1936 Jarrow March is remembered, but not the six much larger Hunger Marches organised by the CP-led NUWM; the heroism and sacrifice of the International Brigade has been subsumed by the biography of George Orwell; and, as Lorna Reith points out in her essay here, the party's huge 1977 'People's Jubilee' is now credited to the SWP. If *Marxism Today* is remembered at all these days, it is as the supposed intellectual midwife to Blairism and the all horrors of New Labour.

This is partly the default position of careless history and popular memory. But it is also the result of an ideologically-driven falsification of the public record that began in the late 1940s with the systematic removal of Communist Party members, first from public life and then from public memory. During the Cold War a number of books were published about the British Communist Party –

notably Gabriel Almond's *The Appeals of Communism* (1954), Henry Pelling's *The British Communist Party* (1958) and Neal Wood's *Communism and British Intellectuals* (1959) – that presented Communist Party members as a chorus-line of knaves and fools, hopeless puppets and deranged utopians. And although a number of more scholarly studies have been published since the party's demise in 1991, they have mostly concentrated on the theoretical debates and their international contexts, or on prosopographical approaches to patterns of belief, commitment and identity.

After the Party represents what we hope will be the beginning of a different kind of conversation, about the felt consequences of the CP's dissolution at a personal and local level. It is not a book about what being a Communist 'meant', but about what not being a Communist means now. These essays look at some of the historical achievements and failures of the party in its last decade in order to consider the consequences for British political and intellectual life of the party not existing during the last twenty years. If it was such a unique and important organisation, why is there so little evidence today that it ever existed at all? Why has no-one re-invented it? Why is there not more of a CP-shaped hole in British life? Was 1991 really the end, or was it the beginning of a different kind of politics? Was it a 'Springtime of the Peoples', or did it signal the demise of participative and representative democracy?

These are questions of more than academic interest. The Communist Party may be history, but the history of its disappearance is highly relevant to any discussion about civil society and popular democracy in Britain, never mind about the future of radical political organisation in the twenty-first century.

These essays do not pretend to constitute a comprehensive answer to these questions. The contributors cannot claim to be typical (whatever that might mean) of the last generation of party members. Twenty years ago we were young activists. Now in middle age, we look back with a mixture of regret, relief and disbelief on the years spent in the party, and reflect on some of the personal, political, and cultural changes of the last twenty years. Each has followed a very different political trajectory – Green Party, Labour Party, CPB, SLP, Respect and no party at all. But none has become a professional anti-communist. And for all the differences of outlook, there are some unexpected consistencies between the stories in this book. Each of the contributors has found other ways of working for change – albeit with more modest ambitions – in local government, in the peace and trades union movements, in journalism, social work, teaching, writing and book-selling. Our political identities are not defined by party affiliation, but by locality, single-issue campaigns, popular culture and literary tradition. We share a commitment to the idea of broad democratic alliances and a deeply-ingrained hostility to managerial and bureaucratic politics. Belonging to the Communist tradition was, if nothing else, an education in the consequences of unbalanced power.

Of course there are many aspects of the party's life which are not included here, other narratives, perspectives and analyses that need to be made. We hope that others will take up some of the arguments made here with arguments and questions of their own. This is just our version of events. But don't take our word for it. As Brecht once put it, 'of all sure things / the surest is doubt.'

Andy Croft
Middlesbrough, November 2011

FURTHER READING

Geoff Andrews, *Endgames and New Times: the Final Years of British Communism 1964-91* (Lawrence and Wishart 2004)
Gidon Cohen, Andrew Flinn and Kevin Morgan (eds), *Communists and British Society 1920-1991: People of a Special Mould* (Rivers Oram Press 2005)
Phil Cohen (ed.), *Children of the Revolution* (Lawrence & Wishart 1997)
Francis Beckett, *Enemy Within; the Rise and Fall of the British Communist Party* (John Murray 1995)
Andy Pearmain, 'Twenty Years On: Whatever Happened to the Communist Party of Great Britain?' *Socialist History* 38, 2011
Neil Rafeek, *Communist Women in Scotland* (Tauris 2008)
Emily Robinson, 'New times, new politics: History and memory during the final years of the CPGB', *British Politics* Vol. 6, 4, 2011
Willie Thompson, *The Good Old Cause: British Communism, 1920-91* (Pluto Press 1992)
Willie Thompson, *The Communist Movement Since 1945* (Blackwell 1998)

The revolution is just a T-shirt away

Mark Perryman

1978. The National Front was attracting votes in by-elections to elevate them into the most serious fascist electoral force since the 1930s heyday of Oswald Mosley's Blackshirts. This was the stuff of primetime news, made all the more spectacular by the mass brawls the NF attracted every time they mustered for an inflammatory march through a multicultural neighbourhood.

In April, Hackney's Victoria Park was the scene of the first Anti-Nazi League and Rock against Racism Carnival. I'd organised a busload of fellow sixth-formers from school to attend, but we were too scared to join the march, and to be honest my persuasive powers didn't stretch much further than the offer of free music. But when Steel Pulse, Tom Robinson, Jimmy Pursey from Sham 69, X-Ray Spex and most of all the Clash burst on to the stage my world was changed for ever, as I'm still proud to say some three decades on.

Rock against Racism and the Anti Nazi League had precious little to do with the Communist Party – they were mainly the inspired invention of the SWP, though the details of who organised what was beyond me at the time. All I knew was that racism mattered, that the NF could be defeated by popular opposition, that rebellion was thrilling, and that politics if it was ever to mean anything to me, or anyone else, had to be pleasurable.

That summer I would pester the Anti Nazi League office for piles of leaflets which I promptly delivered through the letterboxes of my mildly perplexed leafy suburban neighbourhood. Still, if it kept away the threat of the NF jackboots marching down the avenues of Banstead I was surely in the frontline of something important, wasn't I? Another carnival, this time with Elvis Costello, Stiff Little Fingers and Aswad all playing, kept my youthful passion going. The fact that the carnival took place in Brixton convinced me still further that I was definitely in the vanguard of the youth revolt. Surrey had never seemed so far away.

WELCOME TO THE PARTY

In October I started my degree course at Hull University and the choice of which road to follow to the revolutionary overthrow of capitalism proved more bewildering than I'd ever imagined. The Labour Party, Communist Party, SWP and IMG each pressed their wares upon me. Labour proved to be the shortest possible flirtation. Their politics all seemed to be about capturing positions rather than having any depth to their ideals. The SWP were always impressive and had an extraordinary level of commitment, but what they never seemed to appreciate was that their cult of activism repelled far more than they could ever attract. And this was combined with what I soon discovered to be a one-dimensional version of Marxism. As for the IMG, they had both the intellect and the activism, but a decade after 1968 they were chronically confused about what they wanted to do – be a more sophisticated version of the SWP, go for deep entryism into the Labour Party or break out into something new. They could never really decide, and in the end I couldn't be bothered to find out.

While I often found myself coming into contact with the Communist Students in the Broad Left group that was the dominant force in our student union, and liking what I saw, the big attraction for me at that time was the kind of libertarian left politics being articulated at the time around *The Leveller* magazine, and in particular in the socialist-feminist book *Beyond the Fragments* – networking and coalition-building, a critique of the rigidity that democratic-centralism imposed, a rejection of the obsession with party-building and the rush to recruit, and, most of all a feminist critique of a left framed by masculine values and ways of working. Most of this was aimed at the Trotskyist left that the authors of *Beyond the Fragments* had been a part of and now were criticising, but the logic of their critique applied also to the CP.

At the end of my first year as a student I decided to enrol at the annual summer Communist University of London. Gramsci, Poulantzas, listening to Stuart Hall, arguments over hegemony and state power, the economist Sam Aaronovitch making Marxist economics easy to understand, socialist films and rebel music to enjoy. One event I will never forget was a debate between Eric Hobsbawm and miners leader Mick McGahey, on Eric's essay 'The Forward March of Labour Halted?', published in *Marxism Today*. This was entirely different from the sloganising of the Far Left or the self-satisfaction of Labourism. It felt like the arguments and the people taking part really mattered; there was a willingness to honestly and courageously confront the inadequacies of our own politics – what was known as trade union 'sectionalism' – and a recognition that the need to listen to each other was far more important than the issuing of the 'line' for others to follow.

With Thatcher now in power too I returned to Hull in the autumn and promptly joined the CP. My biggest frustration over the next couple of years was what appeared to be the lack of activism of my fellow members compared to our most obvious competitors on campus, the SWP. I gave the branch a largely unwelcome hard time over this, and they were generous enough to listen; and gradually I came to appreciate that thrusting a paper in someone's face, waving a placard, or bawling through a megaphone, might get you noticed and attract a hard core of the politically active, but it didn't necessarily win you many friends beyond that. Ours was a party branch influenced almost as much by feminism as Marxism, and a different way of doing politics was evolving – perhaps not as spectacular as what the Trots could offer, but eventually I learned to appreciate this.

MARX AND SPARKS

At the same time the party's marxism was being challenged too. I'd joined in the autumn of 1979, and this was the time when Martin Jacques initiated the transformation of the Party's 'theoretical and discussion journal' *Marxism Today* into what would eventually become not only a glossy high street magazine but a hugely influential one. *Marxism Today* distinguished itself by trying to understand the reasons why the Tories had won the 1979 election, and criticising the all too obvious inadequacies of the post-war welfare settlement, which the right was now ruthlessly exploiting to their own ends. Treating the failings of the left as a contributory factor towards the Tories' success made the magazine unpopular in a political culture that was and remains woefully defensive. But it also ensured that others, less bound by the unthinking loyalties that both Labourism and Leninism too often demand, wanted to read what the magazine had to say. In a remarkably short space of time *Marxism Today* became relevant, impossible to ignore and always there with something to make you think. The CP meanwhile had an air of being a bit old-fashioned; it had a courageous history, but was not as good at doing the present-day as those bright shiny Trots who at the time were jumping on the punk bandwagon like it was never going out of fashion.

1968, a decade earlier, had been a difficult year. Not only were there the Soviet tanks crushing the Prague Spring to explain away, but in France the students had led the revolt in the face of a French Communist Party that had told them to get back to the classrooms, leaving the class struggle to them. Yet out of this moment it was the communist thinkers Althusser and Gramsci, far more than Trotsky, who would provide the resources that would decisively shape intellectual debate over the next ten years. And the enduring impact of Czechoslovakia for many communists was the socialist democracy of Dubcek not the brutal invasion of Russian power. *Marxism Today* was giving us a platform to promote this dual legacy of '68, even for those like me too young to remember when Paris, London, Rome and Berlin seemed like places where the revolution could win. Yet at the start of 1980, when the left debated the parliamentary versus the revolutionary roads to power in a big gathering in central London dubbed the 'Debate of the Decade', the CP was nowhere to be seen. Tony Benn and fellow left MP Audrey Wise argued Labour's case, with Paul Foot and Tariq Ali representing the Far Left, and the *Beyond the Fragments* authors managing to get a word in between. But the CP? Nobody thought to invite us, and only a few even noticed our absence. *Marxism Today* was to change all that, and not just in these circles; it moved what we had to say into the mainstream. Following Labour's 1983 defeat at the polls, the Labour magazine *New Socialist* published a book of essays, *The Future of the*

Left. Just about every contribution was a response to *Marxism Today*'s analysis of Thatcherism. Meanwhile almost every section of the left became obsessed with denouncing the magazine's supposed revisionism on an almost weekly basis.

CULTURAL REVOLUTIONS

From that first awakening in Victoria Park as the great heaving mass of anti-racist humanity surged around me to the rhythm of the Clash, politics being fun had been a vital part of my activism. But getting it in the neck with accusations of selling out this that and the other that I'd never heard of could hardly be described as a positive experience. And when I was being made to feel responsible for the sins of Stalin committed before I was born, the experience teetered over into the unwelcome, not to mention surreal. *Marxism Today* helped with this. There was nothing else quite like it, and an organisation that just a couple of years previously had seemed irretrievably framed by its past now began to carve out a future for itself. When the CP in the summer of 1980 organised a Beat the Blues Festival at London's Alexandra Palace headlined by punk legends The Slits I couldn't have been happier. This was a cultural politics I thought only existed in continental Europe, where the French and Italian CPs made their festivals truly popular events across the summer months. When Ken Livingstone took control of the GLC he pretty much lifted the entire idea of such events from the CP, and made city park free festivals one of the defining characteristics of his regime. But we'd done it first, and many of us connected the fun we were having to a political practice that was also rooted in Eurocommunism.

None of this, though, had much purchase in Aberdeen, where I next ended up to study for a master's degree. The local CP branch were all convinced Stalinists, mostly members of the Straight Left faction. It was a rude and uncomfortable awakening. When *Marxism Today* regular and prominent socialist feminist Bea Campbell came to the university to give a talk, the crowd was enormous. Hundreds packed in to hear her, but the entire CP branch got up and walked out in disgust when Bea criticised the maleness of most trade unions' practices and priorities. This was also the era of CND and the peace movement, but the Stalinists in Aberdeen wouldn't allow any criticism of the Soviet Union: giving an inch on human rights or Soviet nuclear weapons meant surrendering to imperialism in their warped imaginations, and they exerted almost as much anger against those who led their own party on such alleged misadventures as they did on the powerful forces driving us towards replacing Polaris with Trident missiles and stationing cruise missiles in Britain.

This was the problem at the core of the CP's existence in the 1980s – that it was the home of what were effectively three different and mostly cantankerous parties. The Euros, with whom I vigorously identified. The Stalinists, or Tankies, who would eventually take over the party's newspaper, *The Morning Star*. And in between the centrists, who a lot of the time just wished both of these other lots would leave them alone to get on with the party's business. *Marxism Today* was increasingly regarded with a degree of jealousy by these centrists while the Tankies treated it as nothing less than the class enemy. Not a combination to ensure even a modest level of peaceful co-existence.

If *Marxism Today*'s only achievement had been its success as a glossy high-street magazine, that would have been something: with a few honourable exceptions, the media that the left pours such a huge effort into sustaining is by and large turgid, boring and unreadable for all but those already in the know, especially in terms of its coded jargon. But as the 1980s unfolded, the magazine proved definitively to be something more, much more, than this. It certainly echoed my evolving understanding that if politics was to be effectively transformational rather than to retreat into its own version of conservatism, it required forms that were pre-figurative and plural, a culture that was participative and pleasurable. This was precisely what I found when I headed south from Aberdeen to do a postgraduate certificate of education in Dudley, a town in the West Midlands' Black Country.

A SMALL TOWN CALLED DUDLEY

In Dudley, party members were unusually young, and most had until recently been members of the local Labour Party. The branch was at the centre of just about everything CND did in the town. The

CP's politics of broad alliances, commitment to extra-parliamentary politics and a quite grounded understanding of the centrality of feminism, all combined to fit neatly with a growing movement of massive demonstrations and non-violent women's peace camps. This gained us respect and an audience. We always put the campaign first, instead of shoving a paper or party recruitment form in the face of anybody we came across at the first opportunity. This was a fairly common trait of a kind of selfless communism which was very good at building movements but hadn't a clue what to do with its own party. In Dudley we decided to see if *Marxism Today* could provide us with a form that was more appropriate than the old party branch structure to reach out to an audience that was increasingly interested in the ideas the magazine was now quite well known for. A 'talking shop' was the standard term of derision for our hugely successful efforts in establishing a local *Marxism Today* Discussion Group. Yet much of the left's weakness can be located in its unwillingness to talk, to learn from each other, to host the kind of discussion where you don't know the answer you'll end up with before you begin. Dudley isn't metropolitan in the way London or Manchester is. It is not a university town like Oxford or Lancaster. As we would often proudly write in party publications, if we could do this in Dudley it could be done anywhere. We brought to Dudley the writers behind the articles in the magazine, attracted the kinds of crowds the left in the area hadn't seen in decades, and connected to those who had been buying *Marxism Today* in the local WH Smith, or had read about the magazine because of the increasing coverage it was attracting in the *Guardian* and elsewhere. Of course, in the greater scheme of things this still didn't amount to very much; we're talking tens not hundreds. The Black Country wasn't on the verge of revolution, but the political practice we were experimenting with was vitally important nevertheless. A structure that was far looser than what the CP was used to – no party line, but a culture that revolved around shared ideas and ideals, with a recognition that politics itself had to be remade if any radical change was ever to be achieved. Dudley branch became a kind of symbol for how *Marxism Today* could yet transform, and save, the CP.

Of course what we were getting up to wasn't unique. Across the country *Marxism Today* events, forums and discussion groups were proving increasingly successful – and were posing the question of whether this way of doing our politics could force the change in the CP that it so obviously – to some of us – needed.

Marxism Today wasn't the reason I'd joined the CP – I had signed up just a bit before it went glossy – but it was certainly the reason I remained a member. When I went to work for the magazine in 1986 I joined a team which was incredibly hard-working, paid a pitifully low wage, yet was deeply committed to producing a magazine as professionally as humanly possible despite the most minimal of resources.

NEW TIMES FOR OLD

In 1988 *Marxism Today* achieved what was arguably its greatest ever success. The October issue, coinciding with Labour Party conference, was usually the blockbuster edition, carrying a seminal article with a catchy title in order to attract maximum coverage, provoke reaction, boost sales to their highest for the year. But after Labour's 1987 general election defeat it seemed that the magazine had exhausted almost every possible analysis of the shortcomings of Labourism, and 'Thatcherism' was now firmly established as the *Marxism Today* model for understanding the Conservative government. The rows that had been sparked by the 1984 miners' strike, when the magazine had argued, controversially, that the dispute could not be won by mass pickets alone, were fading fast. It was if we were running out of anything new to say. Up to then the magazine's undoubted strength was critique; a far harder task was to codify the basis of an alternative. But if we could do this, then *Marxism Today* would renew itself and become a core component of any recovery that Labour might be capable of after its third successive defeat at the polls. 'New Times' was the answer – a breathtaking combination of arguments across the themes of post-Fordism, modernity, globalisation, identity politics, power relations and more. The October 1988 edition headline was 'New Times', and the essays it carried still hold their own today as an outstanding resource for an understanding of the political future. For those clinging to the belief that the only option for a defeated left was to modernise, *Marxism Today* provided the answers.

Critically, the party now also became a central part of the debate. Magazine and party had until then existed in a kind of parallel existence; mutually assured reconstruction was anything but guaranteed. The magazine's media coverage was more often than not couched in terms of how strange it was that a Communist Party magazine should be writing these things. If anybody else had done so it would have hardly been worth a mention. Yet there was something deeper than this. The party provided what Martin Jacques described as 'anchorage'. This was what had originally convinced me to join, to be part of an organisation that was greater than the sum of its parts. The CP included in its membership a substantial layer of trade union activists, mostly working-class, and many of them manual workers, and these were genuine worker-intellectuals - 'organic' as Gramsci dubbed them (long before the term became associated with my over-priced vegetables at the local farmers' market). And the fact that *Marxism Today* was a party journal belonging as much to them as to the likes of me represented something important. There was a stake in its fortunes which meant that, though the relationship with the CP could be tense, unhelpful even, it did provide the magazine with a context. And of course that context – for the magazine and the Party – was Marxism. If we drifted away from this we weren't simply defying a conference resolution, we were besmirching a creed. We would become heretics, or, as the lingo went, revisionists. This meant that what the magazine wrote became transcribed on to a much bigger canvas, stretching back to 1917, and beyond to Marx. Engels and *The Communist Manifesto*. Of course, at its worst this could create a cultish sense of our own self importance, out of all proportion to what we represented. Yet, thankfully, that mostly wasn't the case; instead, the anchorage provided by the party created the potential space for shaping the transformation of our own organisation.

'New Times' was the moment when this might have been achieved. The magazine's analysis for the first time was dragged into the mainstream of the party. A draft manifesto was produced. This adapted the New Times ideas, by now attracting an unprecedented depth of interest across the Labour Party, into a strategy to replace the CP's 1977 *British Road to Socialism*, which still acted as the party's kind of all-purpose guide to action. Debate on New Times was now rooted amongst the membership, in the branches and districts; the parallel existences were becoming much closer, and connecting also to a much broader Labour Party rethink. Inevitably the more radical ideas became softened at the edges by the centrists in the party. But the alternative that they offered – a much greater commitment to standing in elections – was hardly a compelling one, given that the votes they achieved were so risible. The centrists resented the success of the *Marxism Today* 'label' at the expense of the CP's identity, but they couldn't come up with anything remotely comparable in terms of attractiveness to a broader left audience. And they moralised too, questioning the value of advertising, marketing and merchandising for progressive politics, as they pored over the magazine to find fault.

1989 AND ALL THAT

After a year of debate, the CP gathered for its Congress in the late autumn of 1989 to establish whether or not the *Manifesto for New Times* was to become the party's strategy for the future. The document was passed, and with only the odd change, but in 1989 it all appeared too late to matter very much any more. With the Berlin Wall crashing around our Communist ears, the horrors of the Chinese Tiananmen Square massacre in the summer, and Christmas a few weeks later celebrated by the ousting of Rumania's brutal Ceausescu, any hope remaining for reform communism, here or anywhere else, seemed exhausted. The magazine survived for another year or so, but the same doubts applied to the continuing worth of having 'Marxism' in the magazine's title. The irony of subverting our founding ideology no longer had the same appeal. Even Gorbachev's *perestroika* had proved incapable of saving communism from itself. Of course us Euros still justified our political identity to ourselves, and others, by way of explaining our opposition to just about everything that Soviet communism ever stood stand for, but the argument was no longer being made with the good faith that had originally framed it.

At the end there were still those who argued that the party should continue as if nothing much had changed. Others made a case for a kind of network of the sort that just a few years earlier the same people had mostly rejected out of hand. Most simply drifted away. I was one of the latter.

In my last couple of years in the CP I'd helped set up another *Marxism Today* group, in Haringey where I was now living. North London was an entirely different proposition to Dudley. The audience in the capital was of course immeasurably bigger for the kind of events we would put on, but we had to compete with a vast range of other attractions, from ICA talks to new variety cabaret, and a constant clash of competing campaign meetings and all varieties of the far left. Many thought what we were trying to do couldn't be done, but just as in Dudley we quickly built up a decent-sized audience putting the cynics to shame in the process. And when the debate on New Times exploded in the autumn of 1988, within a couple of months we put on an event with co-thinkers in Islington, attracting an audience numbering hundreds. Everything once again had pointed to the potential for a different kind of organisation struggling to escape from what the CP had now become.

WHEN THE MUSIC STOPS

With the party over those of us most enthused by *Marxism Today* in and around North London were determined that the legacy of the magazine, and the *Marxism Today* group we had established, shouldn't be squandered. We set up a new kind of discussion group, 'Signs of the Times', committed to developing the key themes of the New Times analysis. We established a kind of twice-yearly series of evening classes in the unlikely, or perhaps likely, surroundings of a Stoke Newington Swedish restaurant. The place was closed on Monday evenings and the owner let us have the run of the place for our sessions. Globalisation, post-Fordism, identity politics and more were eagerly debated over six-week courses. There was no party line, and the meetings were sociable and participative. In our small way we were prefiguring a break with past left practices. Helen Fielding, author of *Bridget Jones's Diary*, joined us one night for a learned discussion of postmodernism. A *Times* journalist, Michael Gove, opened another discussion. I wonder whatever happened to him? The lack of *Marxism Today* meant that we had to develop the ideas for ourselves. We published moderately successful books based on the seminars, and started organising summer conferences too. Eventually, as with any small group, we were exhausted by our efforts and fell apart. If this had all taken part a few years later, when the era of the internet, email, and social networking made this kind of organising so much more practicable, maybe we would have survived. Who knows? But at least we tried and for a decade proved that there remained a space for the kind of politics *Marxism Today* had come to represent, with or without the party.

In 1989 the only sensible response to the collapse of communism appeared to be the dissolution of the CP; and the zeal with which this was pursued by those who now found themselves disbelievers at times resembled that of a moral crusade. *Marxism Today* for a while existed in exile from this fast dissolving CP as it searched around for a new name to describe its politics, but, having failed to find one, it disappeared too. The fact that two decades and a bit later, neither the party nor the magazine have managed to generate any kind of meaningful legacy perhaps suggests that the decisions taken back then were right. But within a few years of the Berlin Wall coming crashing down, circumstances changed domestically and internationally, and raised serious questions marks over that 1989 rush to judgement.

THE BLIAR YEARS

Labour's mid-1990s model of modernisation, Blairism, is often blamed by ill-informed commentators squarely on *Marxism Today* in general, and New Times thinking in particular. The Blairites drew on the description which *Marxism Today* provided of economic, social and cultural change in order to give their old-fashioned Labourist managerialism a shiny new technocratic gloss; while the New Times analysis represented a strategy of transformational politics, as even a cursory reading of the original articles would resolutely prove. However, this wasn't its appeal to Blair's co-thinkers. They simply liked the sense of the newness of what was being described – even while their politics remained old. Nothing very much was changed in actuality. They still viewed their task as being to prove themselves better managers of the state than their opposite numbers across the parliamentary dispatch box. And so New Labour embarked on wholesale privatisation, the demonisation of asylum seekers, the retention of a tax regime beneficial to the rich, a love affair with the business model for running the offices of government, an assault on civil liberties, the marketisation of higher education, and so on. None of this resembled in the least the kind of modernisation New Times had outlined. The scale of disappointment post-1997 was enormous, opening up a political space on the outside left which would have been quite unimaginable less than a decade earlier.

A year after Blair's 1997 victory, following the pattern of many 1980s rock and pop bands, *Marxism Today* reunited for one final gig. A magazine which hadn't existed for almost ten years came storming back with a special, last edition. 'Wrong' was emblazoned across Blair's face on the cover; and all the old favourites, as well as some new authors picked up along the way, wrote inside to re-articulate the *Marxism Today* analysis. This time it was aimed at the corrosive failings of the very Labour government which most of us had fondly believed would be the end of the nightmare of eighteen years of impregnable Tory misrule. Many of those previously most sympathetic to *Marxism Today* inside the Labour Party were now outraged by what they saw as our premature miscalculation. How could a magazine of sophistication rush so recklessly towards such a pessimistic early judgement. Not only were we proved devastatingly correct over the coming months and years, as Blairism dashed just about every hope once bestowed in it, but outside the coteries of old friends and admirers the *Marxism Today* comeback attracted a readership and interest as big as the one we'd left behind in 1990. Just like in the old days I'd been given the circulation job. WH Smith sold out our print run in days and we had to rush out a reprint. The team of volunteers I'd lined up to stuff envelopes with the few mail order copies we thought we'd need to post out were stressed out with the several thousand we had to dispatch. Across the papers and TV debate raged over what we had to say. And then, just as in the best reunions, we packed up our ideological things and departed the stage before we spoilt the moment.

Was that the right thing to do? Should we have stuck around? Who knows? What we can be certain of, is that, after the horrors of 9/11, an illegal war launched on a lie ignited a mass movement of popular revulsion that will stain the reputation of Tony Blair and all who supported him for ever and a day. And those who pleaded

Gordon Brown's case as the alternative were in for a rude awakening when he so rapidly proved not to be much better. But of course *Marxism Today* was no longer around to point any of this out. The odd journalist would proffer a critical piece of some substance. But it was rare indeed to read anything which knitted together anything like an analysis of the sort some of us had become used to from *Marxism Today*.

What did we miss most about *Marxism Today* as New Labour stumbled from one dashing of our hopes to another? It had created a space where intellectualism and journalism combined – underpinned in the main by a critical marxism, but not to the exclusion of other schools of thought, or as part of a misguided defence of the sanctity of the socialist creed. Without such a fusion, and accelerated by the managerialist regime Labour forced upon higher education, these connections evaporated. The Gramscian thesis that 'not all academics are intellectuals' was proved, as the retreat by academics to the comfort of writing solely for their peers turned into a headlong rush. Meanwhile the spaces where the second half of the maxim could take shape – 'and not all intellectuals are academics' – scarcely existed anymore. This was the single most important consequence of nothing taking the place of *Marxism Today*. And the loss was exacerbated by the general absence, with few exceptions, of the kinds of political practice the magazine had pioneered. We also missed the emphasis given to the visual as well as the written contents of the magazine – not the New Labour triumph of style over substance but an understanding that there was absolutely nothing wrong in providing a radical message with attractive packaging. (In fact this was an absolute necessity in the fight for space on the newsstands, and to retain the interest of the general reader.) And we missed the professionalism that had resolutely refused to tolerate the second-rate simply because this was what the resources at our disposal could afford, and this was what we were used to; as well as the recognition and valuing of the particularities of editorial, design, distribution and marketing rather than a privileging of the content; and the breadth of editorial priorities, in recognition that popular culture, the everyday, was a terrain on which ideas were formed, contested and challenged that was every bit as important as the conventional sites of power; and a group of writers, each with their own distinctive contribution to make – built up over a long time but refreshed by new ones periodically – who shared a core set of values but were not restricted to producing a ready-made set of answers; and, most of all, a strategic approach to political change, able to distinguish the tactical necessities of addressing and understanding the here and now, but with a compelling combination of ideas and vision for a better tomorrow.

WEARING OUR HEARTS ON OUR CHESTS

What, if anything, does any of this have to do with T-shirts and football? Rather surprisingly, quite a lot. *Marxism Today* taught me the necessity of rethinking the ways in which we 'do politics', and of remaking the political as an essential component in any process of social change, as well as of acting upon these insights. And the starting point for this is the recognition that the sites where ideas are formed, contested and changed are not restricted either to parliament or protest. The left still can't cope with the fact that its ways of organising, priorities and language bear little or no relevance to the lives and habits of others. The consequences were rather neatly summed by the philosopher of postmodernism Jean Baudrillard – 'Power is only too happy to make football bear a diabolical responsibility for stupefying the masses'. I couldn't have put it better myself. So, with fellow exile from the CP's fallout Hugh Tisdale, we slapped it on a T-shirt and added Baudrillard's name and squad number on the back. Being a postmodernist, a free-floating midfield position seemed strangely appropriate for Baudrillard, one that can swap left for right with bewildering frequency. And the rest is history.

By the mid 1990s, football was acquiring an unprecedented cultural significance, from Nick Hornby's *Fever Pitch* to New Order's 1990 hit *World in Motion*, via Baddiel and Skinner's *Fantasy Football*. We never had a masterplan, but our Philosophy Football T-shirts kind of fitted in with this mood, as Camus, Sartre, Bob Marley and Simone de Beauvoir lined up with the likes of Best, Cruyff and the best-selling t-shirted manifesto of Bill Shankly – 'The socialism I believe in is everyone working for each other, having a share of the rewards. It's the way I see football, the way I see life.' Why shouldn't wearing ideas on our chest be every bit as important in terms of effecting change as reading about them in a book?

The 1977 programme of the CP, *The British Road to Socialism*, pioneered the idea and practice of the 'broad democratic alliance'. Stretching back to the 1930s Popular Front against Fascism, which managed to include vicars, Liberals and even Tories in opposition to the Blackshirts, Franco's Spain and the Nazis, the CP had always been in favour of building the broadest possible coalitions. How might this apply to selling football T-shirts? There are plenty of small companies who more or less do the same, but what makes Philosophy Football different is the mix. We appeal to club fans, and fans of England, and to those who prefer their football with a more internationalist flavour. We daub philosophers' quotes about football on a shirt, and appeal mainly to intellectuals and students, the type who read *London Review of Books*, but depict the quote in a way that might appeal to anyone who just likes the wit and wisdom of the quote and the design. And then there's our 'dissenter' range – from anti-BNP and pro-Palestine to Cuba Solidarity, from a republican alternative to the Royal Wedding hoopla to opposition to the cuts. We certainly don't disguise our ideals and the causes we support, but in true Popular Frontist style we don't make sharing these with us as a condition of purchase either. It is this combination which helps make Philosophy Football unique. Who would ever have imagined that a grounding in creative Marxism could form the basis of a small business's niche-marketing success?

This is perhaps most obvious with the 'soft patriotism' which Philosophy Football has virtually invented – making the distinction between a pride in the team, and the prejudice that sometimes accompanies it, refusing to accept the former is impossible without the latter. Boisterously proclaiming that whoever you are, wherever you come from, whatever your faith or none, we can all be England if we choose to be.

Philosophy Football began in 1994, with a simple Christmas present idea for our friends, then friends of friends, and not much more. But within two years England was hosting Euro 96, *Three Lions on My Shirt* became a fans' anthem, and an England shirt our unofficial national dress, while the St George Cross was absolutely everywhere. Across England it has been pretty much the same every other summer since. Today it is becoming more acceptable to combine the progressive and the patriotic, but in the mid-1990s this was much less the case. Gramsci's writings on the 'national-popular' had always made me uncomfortable with those varieties of Marxism which treated nationalism and internationalism as polar opposites. Why shouldn't any right-thinking person combine the two? Eric Hobsbawm and Stuart Hall wrote powerfully in *Marxism Today* on this subject in the aftermath of the Falklands War, carefully unpicking English patriotism's cause from the excesses of jingoism. The work of the CP Historians Group on the English Civil War remains probably British Marxism's most influential intellectual legacy, and E.P. Thompson's *The Making of the English Working Class* is a classic of both historiography and marxist writing too. No, we didn't try to squeeze all of this lot on to a T-shirt – though Hobswbawm's dictum summing up why a team dressed in England shirts has had such an impact on modern formations of national identity – 'the imagined community of millions seems more real as a team of eleven named people' – did make it on to one of our designs.

There was another part of *Marxism Today*'s practice that influenced Philosophy Football too. The left's antipathy towards the media often encourages a wilful ignorance of how it works. Of course getting a plug here, a word in edgeways there, doesn't change or challenge the fact of control of the media by monopolisation and corporate power. But nor should it prevent us from using every possible outlet we can persuade to give us any coverage we can manage. In our early days Philosophy Football was so quirky that we got a lot more column inches and airtime than an outfit of our size really merits, and we took every possible advantage of this, playing up the eccentricities of the philosophy and football combination for all they were worth. *Marxism Today* had been the same, taking the media seriously, realising that any mentions the magazine could earn would reach hundreds of thousands, millions even, compared to the measly numbers we were more used to communicating with. Understanding how the media works rather than being against it almost as a point of principle (and then wondering why next to no coverage is forthcoming) became a key part of how Philosophy Football operated.

Design identity was also vital to *Marxism Today* – although it was the Labour Party magazine *New Socialist* which originated the term 'designer socialism' in the 1980s and began the slow descent into spin doctor ship which this eventually justified. For *Marxism Today* the visual was important, but was itself part of a political project rather than divorced from it. This was a necessity for a magazine that needed to grab attention on the packed shelves of a newsagent. And the densely written discussion pieces needed an accompanying visual narrative if they were ever to be read beyond a very limited audience of the most intellectually engaged and politically committed. In a similar way Philosophy Football is a partnership between the verbal and the visual. Marketing and design are each equally vital to our success. Of course there have been episodes in the left tradition when the visual has been taken seriously. But these remain relatively uncommon and have a habit of then establishing a house style which, while revolutionary at the point of origination, swiftly becomes fixed, unable to adapt to the surrounding visual landscape which is constantly changing. Philosophy Football's co-founder and designer Hugh Tisdale often describes his contribution to the company as being its 'eyes and ears' while I am the 'mouth' – by that I think he means I'm a bossy self-publicist and he's a visual artist. But the relationship works, reflecting the need to break with the left's privileging of the written word and speechifying at the expense of almost any other means of communication.

The combination of words and visuals with an exploration of communicating via the other senses – touch, taste and smell – lies at the centre of the events Philosophy Football has pioneered, 'parties with a purpose'. These are heavily influenced by the kinds of political and cultural weekend-long extravaganzas organised by *Marxism Today*, plus the heritage of the CP festivals and the Communist University of London. Why shouldn't ideas be entertaining? Why can't politics be pleasurable? Our parties mix film and photography, comedy with poetry, music and dance, food and drink, while having the discussion of ideas at the centre of the evening too. It is easy enough to put on a benefit night style of evening, but creatively connecting the ideas to the entertainment is a much harder, although infinitely more rewarding, task. And we go further than this. The poet, the comic, the musician is as much a communicator of ideas as the fifteen-minute speech; a party is a better way to bring people together for the cause than a conference; and the commitment and imagination inspired or renewed are longer lasting than anything most rallies are likely to generate.

A FINAL ACT

Many years after the CP dissolved and I'd left, a final act was committed by the remaining ex-CP members in the successor organisation they had set up which can only be described as gross negligence. They disposed of all the CP's remaining, and not inconsiderable, financial and capital assets, mainly property. Those assets were given away to an ineffectual electoral reform group, 'Unlock Democracy', which virtually nobody will have heard of before or since, and incorporates the last bare bones of Charter 88. It was perfectly true, as some argued, that a proportion of these riches were ill-gotten Moscow Gold and the like, but goodness only knows what giving them away to those with no connection at all to the CP was supposed to achieve. In my opinion the right to make that decision didn't belong to just the few who had set up Democratic Left and its successor organisations. The assets could have been tied up in a trust, or helped form the basis of some kind of grant-giving body – a recognition that this was what remained, for good and ill, of where the CP had come from was the honest outcome of dissolution, not this self-defeating act of disposal.

THE OUTSIDE LEFT SINCE 1991

Circumstances change. 2011, two and a bit decades on from the 'end of communism', opened with the 'Arab Spring'. Of course, Egypt and Tunisia are not the crucibles of a new 1917, but they certainly prove definitively that the dynamic of rebellion has not been extinguished. The War on Terror provoked a mass movement that dwarfed CND even at its height, with the crucial difference that this was a campaign in which the mainly white left marched alongside and shared the leadership with those of a different colour skin and different faith. For all the posturing of anti-racism this had never happened before, though it led some on the left to indulge in a wilful misunderstanding of Islam – comparable to the Islamophobes on the right. Difference demands dialogue and exchange; the rabid imposition of uniformity based on a single leftist code does not work and never did.

Ten years after 1989, the scale of disappointment in the Blair government had spread so rapidly and so widely that it created a space for an outside left of some substance. Government reforms had introduced PR at the Scottish and Welsh parliamentary and assembly elections, and in the European and Greater London elections. This opened the possibility for small parties to get elected via a much more representative system. In the Scottish Parliament the Scottish Socialist Party (SSP) achieved the biggest electoral breakthrough for a left of Labour party since the CP's two MPs were elected in 1945 – initially with Tommy Sheridan's election in the first elections, and then in the next with six MSPs. Only for the party to fall apart in the most spectacular of fashion with allegation and counter-allegation concerning Tommy Sheridan's sex life, the high court, libel and perjury. A terrible end to an episode that at least showed what was still possible for a political project beyond Labour.

In London the victory of Ken Livingstone in the 2000 London Mayoral election, standing as an independent left candidate against the official Labour candidate, also revealed the possibilities that were emerging. Livingstone's mid-1980s version of municipal socialism was probably the closest thing inside Labour to the kind of civic change that had developed in cities such as Bologna when it was governed by the Italian Eurocommunists. But Livingstone has never had any kind of project to transform the Labour Party itself; local government for him is the tool for social change, not the party. And so despite his victory from outside the party machine, it was no surprise that he didn't use the opportunity he had so successfully created to found at least in London some kind of alternative to Labour. Instead, almost as quickly as he had left he rejoined Labour.

When George Galloway defeated the odiously pro-war Oona King in Bethnal Green and Bow at the 2003 general election, his achievement matched Phil Piratin's when he won the same constituency as a communist candidate in the 1945 general election. This had been the Communist Party's electoral high point. But Piratin's victory had been backed by an organisation with tens of thousands of members, a network of full-time activists, a party press, and an internal culture with roots in working-class communities the like of which we've never seen experienced since. Galloway's victory was always unlikely to be repeated. And despite the Labour left's outspoken opposition to the war (which in Galloway's case had led to his expulsion), and despite its sharing almost nothing in common with Labour's forward march rightwards under Blair, not a single MP, hardly any councillors and not many members joined Galloway when he left. Perhaps the MPs preferred the cosy sinecure of guaranteed electoral survival, despite standing for a party with which they were now in wholesale disagreement. The members were probably simply too disillusioned to join anything else. Galloway's party, Respect, is now led by Salma Yaqoob, the hijab-wearing former Birmingham councillor. Without Galloway's baggage of personality-led politics, her achievements are perhaps even more impressive. Yet the party she leads is now not much more than a shell.

The economic crash of 2007 re-awakened an interest in questioning the way capitalism worked. The system no longer seemed as impregnable, beyond question, as it had back in 1989. Marx's *Capital* was back in fashion as a textbook to help understand the mess we were now in. Yet all that appears left are those same 'fragments' that the authors who first influenced me had written about in 1979. This process of fragmentation was immeasurably accelerated by the reaction to 1989, and then again by the dashed hopes of the 1997 New Labour triumph. The failings of the SSP, Livingstone and Respect were each tied up in their different ways with variants of Trotskyism, the Militant Tendency, Socialist Action and the SWP. Once the bitter but very much junior rivals of the CP, Militant (now renamed the Socialist Party) and the SWP have since 1989 become effectively mini-me CPs. They are no longer obsessed with the question of how to classify the failings of Soviet communism (state capitalist? degenerate workers state? bureaucratic collectivism?) but both organisations still cling to the trappings of classic Leninism for all they are worth, and so remain trapped in the kind of time warp the CP was incapable of escaping.

It is hard to imagine what will become of the CP's tradition, ideas and practices once the last surviving memories pass into history.

Outside of Britain not a single other CP dissolved itself in quite the same way. Across Europe, in Greece, France and Spain, Communist Parties remain significant social and political forces. Their fortunes ebb and flow but they certainly still matter. In Italy for a while the 'Refoundation' version of the PCI forged an alliance with anti-globalisation protesters with impressive results both on the streets and at the ballot box. That moment has now passed, but the party persists. In Germany, the Left Party has united former Social Democrats and former Communists to secure a series of hugely impressive electoral victories. Other variants of successful opposition parties beyond Labour can be found in the Netherlands, and the Scandinavian Green Left parties which emerged post-1989. And in Portugal, while the CP survives, it has begun to be overshadowed by a more creative Left Bloc of a Trotskyist and Maoist background, but not limited in the least by these early influences. In 2011 in Ireland the United Left Alliance, which mixes community activism with traditional Trotskyist politics, secured the election of the largest number of outside left TDs to the Irish Parliament for a generation. Perhaps most remarkably of all, Communist Parties even survive in the former Warsaw Pact countries, where mass unemployment, increasing inequality, and the break-up of social solidarity has led many to question just how good the new days are, even if they are not calling for a return to the bad old days before 1989.

Does any of this add up – despite the CP no longer being around to witness it – to the revolution being 'just a T-shirt away'? Probably not. But whilst we're waiting, I do at least know a bloke who will sell you the shirt. And if anybody asks him, are you now or have you ever been, he'll answer, proudly and defiantly. Yes, a Communist.

A political error of vast proportions

Kate Hudson

For me, it all began with class. My grandfather, Percy Hudson, worked in the coke ovens at Horden Colliery in County Durham. My father spoke of Percy's brothers working underground in the narrow coal seams five miles out under the North Sea, lying in spaces only eighteen inches deep, often in water. The physical strain of the work led to their early deaths, in their late thirties or early forties, mostly of heart attacks. Percy was the lucky one. He worked on the surface and survived into his sixties. If class identity can be a primordial instinct, class solidarity an emotional compulsion, then I've got it in the very fibre of my being. For Percy and many others in that community, class meant the union, whether of miners, mechanics or cokemen. The union was a matter of dignity and pride, which dominated life, from the pit, to the miners' hall, to Horden 'Big Club' – the working men's club – and even to the ballot box. For class also meant the Labour Party – and union and party were so interlinked they were often indistinguishable. The party dominated politics at every level and was fundamental to the people's lives, representing them and their advancement. My uncle Fred was constituency agent for Emmanuel Shinwell, who had taken the local Easington constituency from Ramsay MacDonald in 1935, and held it until his retirement in 1970. Communists were a rare, eccentric 'other'. The Durham mining village Chopwell was known as Little Moscow because of its strong support for the Communist Party, boasting street names such as Marx Terrace and Lenin Terrace. But Chopwell was very much the exception that proved the rule.

My father, Tom Hudson, broke away from the pit. Percy was one factor in this – no miner wanted his son to go down the pit, and the union's emphasis on education and the advancement of the working class made the goal of further education and alternative aspirations possible. Percy and his wife Jenny worked to ensure that Tom stayed on at school until eighteen rather than leaving at fourteen or fifteen as others did during the 1930s. Instead he went to Sunderland Art College. The other factor was the war. Tom was called up in 1940, fighting in Burma, experiencing battlefield horrors at Kohima, and the suffering and loss which profoundly shaped him, as it no doubt did all those who survived, having seen their comrades blown to pieces. But at least as powerful in its political impact was his experience – having, unusually, survived two years at the Burma front – when he was sent on leave to Calcutta. This was during the Great Famine, the 'man-made' famine, where thousands lay dead and dying of starvation in the streets. The famine was the result of the manipulation of the price of rice, and the guilt was at the door of the British imperial masters. The combined experience of Burma and Calcutta reinforced Tom's anti-war and anti-imperialist views and he held them strongly throughout his life. But he never joined a party or became politically active in the conventional sense. After the war he went back to art college and eventually entered a career as both an artist and an art educator. But his politics was fundamental and shaped my world view significantly.

When I eventually joined the Communist Party, he told me that he had read and sold *Labour Monthly* – edited by that formidable anti-colonialist, Rajani Palme Dutt – with friends from the Young Communist League, and had been chased by fascists as he did so. What I didn't know until much later was that he thought the Russian revolution was the most important event in human history. I don't suppose he ever described himself as a communist, but without doubt his humanity – and his confidence in humanity to advance – were absolutely shaped by his class and anti-imperialist values. On a more practical level, it was his visit to the Soviet Union which meant that I first met the little yellow booklet that was *The Communist Manifesto*, and became acquainted with Soviet-produced Lenin pamphlets.

The Communist Manifesto was a revelation to me. Such clarity of thought, such principle – and such common sense. I can honestly say that since my first teenage reading of *The Communist Manifesto*, I have never looked back. It has shaped my view of both class and party. Not only the necessary role of the working class in the universal emancipation of humanity, but the *sine qua non* of communists – to have no interests separate and apart from those of the working class. What better call to arms against sectarianism than that? What clearer guide to action in every political decision or dilemma?

My father's other political gift was to help me understand that the real driver for change was love of humanity not class hatred. For many years as a child, this was literally conveyed to me in a completely visual way. On a poster on my father's bathroom wall was a photograph of Che Guevara with his simplest yet most profound statement: 'Let me say, at the risk of seeming ridiculous, that the true revolutionary is guided by great feelings of love'.

JOINING THE PARTY

So it was that when I went to university in 1977, the first thing I wanted to do was join the Communist Party. I'd already had some exposure to it at school – a friend's parents were members and I had read the *Morning Star* and been to a party event. This was a celebration of the fifty-ninth anniversary of the Russian revolution held at Wimbledon Town Hall, featuring Harry Gold and his Pieces of Eight – a popular dance band that quite extraordinarily enhanced the mystique of the communists for a seventeen-year-old schoolgirl. My attempts to belong now hit the first hurdle. When I entered the freshers' fayre in my first year at university, the Communist Society stall was staffed by rather older sophisticated students talking amongst themselves. I was much too shy to make the approach. A moment later I passed the Labour Club stall, where a friendly young woman pressed me into not-totally unwilling membership. After all, although Labour was not my goal, nevertheless it was safe, it was family.

Of course student life in the late 1970s was affected by a wide range of cultural and political factors: from punk to Baader-Meinhof and the catastrophe of the attempts to import guerrilla tactics into western urban political conflict; from the apparently unchallengeable power of the trade unions to the onset of Thatcherism that would smash militant labour and the left in a brutal class battle; and the impact of the simultaneously empowering and potentially fragmenting upsurge of the struggles for black, women's and gay liberation. As my university years progressed, the attraction of the more radical leftist groups was strong. The International Marxist Group – a post-1968 orthodox Trotskyist organisation – was by far the most theoretically developed, and particularly attractive to me around the questions of feminism and what is now called identity politics. The SWP student organisation was noisy and enthusiastic, with deceptively simple answers to complex problems. But they really ruled themselves out for me because of their fence-sitting position during the Cold War – neither Washington nor Moscow but international socialism. What did that mean when the fundamental struggle was against imperialism? It meant dead-end contortions over crystal clear issues like Korea and Vietnam.

My final decision on political affiliation came in 1979. Enough of the victories were still with us for me to feel that the movement was in a state of advance, not facing imminent defeat on a massive scale. At that time the Communist Party had getting on for 30,000 members. It was a major political player in numerous ways. Where, I asked myself, would the working class go politically, if there was a further turn to the left in Britain? Would it be the IMG or the SWP? No, I concluded, it would be to the Communist Party. And so I joined.

Prior to the dissolution of the Soviet Union, the different elements of the left were largely defined by their analysis of and attitude to, the Soviet Union. 1991 changed all that, and a very different left political landscape began to emerge, where the fault lines were redrawn, and from the wreckage emerged new left, anti-capitalist forces, usually built around the Communist Parties, or lefts of Communist Parties that had not capitulated to capitalism or seamlessly morphed themselves into social democracy. The situation in Britain was actually quite unusual – that a CP should wind itself up and abandon the marxist project for human liberation. Elsewhere, communists rose better to the challenge of taking the principles forward in a new political context. The Communist Party had been an anchor to the left in British politics, and with its dissolution a small yet extremely significant part of the political landscape was vacated and has not yet been filled. The role of the Communist Party as the far left of the political mainstream, with its capacity to lead, innovate and influence, through its relations with the trade unions, civil society organisations and campaigns – not to mention the left of the Labour Party – stood in stark contrast to the marginal and isolated positions of the ultra-left organisations. The leadership of the Communist Party, which chose to terminate that historic role, dealt a body blow to left politics in Britain, and also ensured that the British working-class movement would not only be devoid of any effective leadership, but would also stand outside the positive left political developments which were to take place in western Europe in the 1990s. These were largely in the orbit of communist parties that were looking for new ways of taking forward marxist politics, rather than attempting to consign them to the dustbin of history as the British party leadership had done.

It always struck me as particularly reprehensible that a number of those who had chosen to lead our party – and would clearly already have known about any crimes and misdemeanours perpetrated by our party or any other – should have gone into an agony of political self-flagellation in 1989, and seen it almost as a moral duty to wind up the party. This was to fail to understand the political role of the Communist Party and the historical necessity for it in the advancement not only of the working class but of humanity as a whole. That in turn led to a failure to understand the real significance of the events of 1989 and 1991, and what action was actually necessary as a result. In the view of many communists and others on the left who remained committed to the revolutionary transformation of society in the interests of the whole of society, the defeat of the Soviet Union was a catastrophic event for humanity and the way forward was clear. It was essential to regroup and rebuild the international workers' movement. Others could choose to give up, to capitulate to capitalism and many did – like much of the party leadership – succumbing to the ahistorical nonsense peddled at that time, like the 'end of history' thesis of Francis Fukuyama, who argued that the very process of historical change was now over, because capitalism had 'won'. Even the most cursory survey of the last twenty years exposes that as triumphalist drivel not worth the paper it was written on.

So why did I take the view that the way forward for humanity lay with the organised movement of the working class, when so much appeared to suggest that the attempt to build workers' states had been a failure? And beyond that, if those states had failed, why did I think their collapse was catastrophic? For me, the answer lay in one of the most basic propositions of marxism: because the victory of the working class is the necessary and fundamental step in 'universal human emancipation', each advance of the international working class benefits the whole of humanity. And every major defeat of the working class will throw back not only that class, but the whole of human civilisation and culture. This is something that the Communist Party leadership had lost sight of. I well remember talking with one leading member towards the end of the party who insisted that the party should not prioritise class as an 'oppression' over other 'oppressions'. This led to the worst kind of shopping-list politics, but more importantly missed the fundamental point about the working class and its potential historical role in liberating society as a whole, not just itself. It was that relationship between the working class and the future of society that was the basis of Marx's socialism. In Marx's view, a class could only lead society if it represented not only its own interests but the wider interests of society. As Marx wrote in *The German Ideology*: 'The class making a revolution comes forward from the very start ... not as a class but as the representative of the whole of society, as the whole mass of society confronting the ruling class ... Its victory, therefore, benefits also many individuals of other classes which are not winning a dominant position ... Every new class, therefore, achieves domination only on a broader basis than that of the class ruling previously...' But, having achieved the leadership of society, the ability of previous leading classes to represent wider interests of society – their universality in Marx's expression, or hegemony in Lenin's – was limited and ultimately negated by conflict between their particular interests and the further development of society.

So, the great bourgeois revolutions of the eighteenth century, by striking down feudalism, advanced not only the bourgeoisie but also all other classes oppressed by feudal social relations. However, after 1848, the class interests of capital more and more conflicted with the general development of society. The result was increasingly violent economic and political upheavals which culminated in the world wars of the twentieth century. From that point on, far from representing the universal interests of human civilisation and culture, capital threatened to extinguish them. This then posed the question of what class could prevent the progressive advances which humanity had made from being destroyed – like limited franchise, limited labour rights, limited education and so on. Indeed, what could advance them?

The answer was given in Russia's October 1917 revolution, taking that country out of the First World War and providing an objective base of support for every subsequent struggle against capitalism and imperialism. The Russian revolution demonstrated in practice the historical role of the working class which had been theorised by Marx seventy years earlier. This is from volume six of the *Collected Works*:

> All preceding classes that got the upper hand, sought to fortify their already acquired status by subjecting society at large to their conditions of appropriation. The proletarians cannot become masters of the productive forces of society, except by abolishing their own previous mode of appropriation, and thereby also every other mode of appropriation. They have nothing of their own to secure and fortify … All previous historical movements were movements of minorities or in the interests of minorities. The proletarian movement is the self-conscious, independent movement of the immense majority in the interests of the immense majority. The proletariat, the lowest stratum of our present society, cannot stir, cannot raise itself up, without the whole superincumbent strata of official society being sprung in the air.

So for Marx, the working class was the most universal class in history, because the accomplishment of its specific class goals necessitated not only the liberation of itself but the liberation of the whole of humanity. But, to accomplish its historic role the working class has to become organised and conscious of it. As Trotsky put it, in *In Defence of Marxism*: 'The Marxist comprehension of historical necessity has nothing in common with fatalism. Socialism is not realisable "by itself", but as a result of the struggle of living forces, classes and their parties. The proletariat's decisive advantage is the fact that it represents historical progress, while the bourgeoisie incarnates reaction and decline.'

So for me this was absolutely fundamental. Only the working class can emancipate humanity – it cannot be done by the bourgeoisie, the radical intelligentsia, nice people wanting to organise a 'good society', or some inchoate new notion like 'multitude'. But that emancipation is not going to happen by magic. It requires the working class to be organised and conscious of its role. That had always been the challenge for communists and that remains so today. It is not surprising then that I consider the dissolution of the CPGB to have been a political error of such vast proportions.

POST-1991

Thus the need since 1991 to work for left regroupment to advance the working class and ultimately the whole of society has been an absolutely clear goal for me as well as many others. For myself, there have been two ways in which I have been engaged with it. The first is with the wider European process which has largely taken place in a political party context which I have had some engagement with, both as an academic working in that field and in relation to my own position as a former leading activist in the CPGB and subsequently a member of the Communist Party of Britain. The second is in what I have seen as a *de facto* realignment process which has taken place in Britain, primarily outside and often in spite of the party political structure, namely the anti-war movement after 9/11.

The former development, the post-1991 European left realignment process, has occupied a large part of my theoretical and practical political work over the last twenty years. It is not widely recognised or understood by the left in Britain, who are generally obsessed by the minutiae of their own relations with other marginal forces, so it needs to be elaborated upon here. Unlike in Britain, a new European left emerged in the early 1990s and went on to have some considerable success in a number of key European states – France, Germany, Spain and Italy, amongst others – playing a role in, or in support of, national or regional governments. This left could be simply described as a converging political current of Communist Parties, former CPs and other parties to the left of social democracy. But it was also a complex process and from a communist point of view, part of its significance was that it embraced only one part of the communist movement.

From 1989 it was possible to see three trajectories which communist parties – or sections of them – variously followed. Firstly, those who chose the path to social democracy, exemplified by the majority grouping within the Italian Communist Party (PCI) and often favoured by those from the Eurocommunist tradition. The majority in the leadership of the CPGB – although not of the membership – was enamoured with the PCI, and followed the 'transformation' route. The balance of forces being what it was, this actually meant that the CPGB became a bizarre think-tank on the road to radical Blairism, hung up on tactical voting and other matters irrelevant to universal human emancipation.

Secondly, there were those parties who failed to recognise the new political situation, or whose response to it was to dig in and defend the old traditions. The key mistake was to think that the essence of communism was defined by tradition and formula rather than by how actually to advance the anti-imperialist struggle in the current moment, and that this might involve the same principles but different strategy, tactics and methods. In reality these parties often became nostalgic communist sects, living in the past, tied to a disappearing electorate and in irreversible decline.

The third category, which is the one that has actually had a positive impact on economic and social struggles and advanced the working class over the past twenty years, was made up of those parties that formed the new European left and which had two particularly significant characteristics. Whether or not they retained the name communist, they certainly retained a commitment to marxist politics, to an anti-capitalist perspective, taking account of the realities of European and world politics at the end of the twentieth century. Many also showed a considerable capacity for open political debate and renewal, drawing on and opening up to feminism, environmental and anti-racist politics. But most unusually, in many cases these parties either initiated, or participated in, a realignment of left forces, often working with organisations that would previously have been regarded as politically hostile. This included allying with or even merging with the electorally insignificant, but very active, new left organisations – often based on a Trotskyist political orientation

– which had expanded dramatically after 1968. Such groups participated in Spain's United Left, merged with the left wing of the Italian Communist Party to found the Party of Communist Refoundation, were included in the electoral lists of Germany's Party of Democratic Socialism (PDS) and eventually joined its successor party, Die Linke, and were invited to participate in common actions and debates initiated by the French Communist Party.

Before 1989, such cooperation would have been inconceivable, but the defeat of the Soviet Union also had a significant impact on much of the mainly Trotskyist and other new left parties that had emerged from the 1968 radicalisation in Europe. Some of those drifted off to the right, but many, whilst being left critics of the Soviet Union, concluded that its overthrow by capitalism was a disaster, and they were prepared to work with communist parties and their successors in the post-Soviet world on the basis of an anti-capitalist and anti-imperialist perspective. Disagreements about the Spanish civil war seemed less pressing than the neoliberal onslaught on the welfare state and the formerly colonial world. This approach was encapsulated by PDS Chair Lothar Bisky at the party's Fourth Congress held in January 1995: '… together we want to tap and use the ideas of communists such as Rosa Luxemburg, Karl Liebknecht, Nikolai Bukharin, the old Leon Trotsky or Antonio Gramsci. It is undisputed that we commemorate those communists who were persecuted and killed by the fascists. Yet it is also our duty to honour those who were killed by Stalin'.

The forerunner of the new European Left was Izquierda Unida (IU), the United Left, in Spain. Its early development was the result of the particular conditions in Spain following the demise of Franco's dictatorship and the early collapse of the Spanish Communist Party (PCE) as a result of the Eurocommunist policies of the late 1970s. It originated in the campaign against Spain's membership of NATO, which was the subject of a nationwide referendum in 1986. A broad committee, which included communists, pacifists, feminists, human rights groups, Christians and the far left – but not the former Eurocommunist PCE leader Santiago Carrillo, who refused to participate – coordinated a vigorous anti-NATO campaign. In spite of media saturation and huge pressure for a Yes vote, it won 43 per cent of the vote. This anti-NATO campaign provided the basis for the founding of IU in 1986. Its main components were communists, left dissidents from PSOE – the Spanish socialists, the Republican Left, and some smaller left groupings, subsequently including members of the Trotskyist Fourth International. Initially it made little advance on the PCE's election result of 1982, but by October 1989 it had more than doubled its vote with 9.1 per cent of the vote. The political composition of IU became something of a pattern in the shaping of the new European left over the subsequent years. The parties of this new current have made a significant impact on western Europe over the past twenty years and have been the chief exponents – and achievers – of advances for the working class and the population more broadly, whether it be the achievement of the thirty-five hour week in France or a range of other socially progressive legislation in the context of socialist, environmental, gender, race and human rights policies.

Unfortunately Britain has been outside this new mainstream of the European left because of the absence of a communist party willing to face the realities of building an alternative vision and reality of a socially solidaristic Europe. The nearest we have seen to the European attempts to transcend previous divisions and build a new political entity to address the new political context that we have faced, particularly in the last ten years, has been the Respect Party. Respect was an attempt to build a new political coalition based around some of the forces which brought the anti-war movement to national prominence and indeed to global significance. Its outstanding achievement was to draw sections of the Muslim community that had been radicalised by the Iraq war into a wider socially progressive coalition with elements of the far left. But Respect was unable to make a major break into significant political and electoral support, partly – it would appear to an outsider – due to tensions within and between its far left components. But it was eminently understandable that such an initiative would take place, given the extraordinary range of social and political forces that were brought together by the anti-war movement in the years following 9/11. My own involvement in the leadership of the anti-war movement came about as a result of my position in the Campaign for Nuclear Disarmament (CND).

CND

In the years after 1991, the absence of the CPGB, for which I had worked as well as being a member and activist, left me in search of a new political focus in which to invest my energies. Whilst I engaged in a number of campaigning activities, it was only really towards the end of the decade that I finally found the issue which was to motivate me as intensely and comprehensively as the Communist Party had done – the struggle for peace and, in particular, against nuclear weapons. Like hundreds of thousands of others I had protested against cruise missiles in the early 1980s, straying into the orbit of CND, as well as spending time at Greenham, that iconic and life-changing assault on male militarism which was in turn subject to brutal political and physical attack by the British state. Like most of those mobilised against nuclear weapons in the 1980s, I strayed back out of the issue after 1989 as the end of the Cold War made us think that nukes had somehow gone away.

But as the 1990s progressed it became clear that we were not witnessing a new world order of peace and global harmony. Whilst the Warsaw Pact had been wound up, NATO had not, and indeed was in the process of expansion. Just days before the first regime-change war masquerading as 'humanitarian war' – NATO's attack on Yugoslavia in 1999 – three former Warsaw Pact countries, Poland, Hungary and the Czech Republic, were admitted to NATO. At the same time the US was pursuing 'national missile defence', a new iteration of Reagan's Star Wars system of the early 1980s, designed to give it the ability to end the strategic balance between the US and Russia by ending the threat of mutually assured destruction. If the US were to launch a first strike attack against Russia, the missile defence system would be able to knock out what was left of Russia's retaliatory forces. Not surprisingly Russia reacted very negatively to the development of missile defence, as the Soviet Union had done in the 1980s, and as it continues to do today, in response to Obama's more subtle version of the system. The end result of these developments was that I became involved in CND, first as Chair of London Region CND and then as a national vice-chair – a post to which I was elected in September 2001, just days after 9/11. The context of our anti-nuclear campaigning was transformed fundamentally, and

CND took its place in the leadership of a new anti-war movement, working not only to prevent a disastrous war, but to take nuclear weapons campaigning out of its ghetto and into a public understanding that nuclear weapons are about war – that they are not just a particularly nasty piece of military kit. And of course engagement in the anti-war movement also meant introducing a radicalising new generation to our nuclear issues too, and brought CND thoroughly into the twenty-first century.

Of course for me as a communist, anti-war campaigning was in my political blood. The origins of the communist movement lay in the struggle against imperialist war in 1914, and the fundamental principle of international working-class solidarity originating in Marx and Engels's statement in the Communist Manifesto, 'Communists everywhere support every revolutionary movement against the existing social and political order of things ... Let the ruling classes tremble at a communist revolution. The proletarians have nothing to lose but their chains. They have a world to win. Working men of all countries, unite!' The communist view, which I continue to hold, is that workers have a bond with class not nation, and therefore their allegiance and interest lies with international proletarian solidarity and not with support for their national bourgeoisies.

The origins of the communist movement were to be found in defence of this principle against the majority of the workers' movement in the context of the First World War. During the years of the Second International, founded in 1889, all kinds of debates had developed, around reform and revolution, around the participation of working-class parties in bourgeois governments – not an abstract debate given the rise of the massive marxist-based Social Democratic Party in Germany. But by the end of the first decade of the twentieth century, after a wave of increasing radicalisation which included the 1905 Russian revolution and general strikes in Western Europe for universal suffrage, divisions began to emerge within the Second International. The declaration of war on 14 August 1914 finally separated the revolutionaries, such as Lenin in Russia and Rosa Luxemburg and Karl Liebknecht in Germany, from revisionists such as Karl Kautsky.

The Second International tradition had been anti-militarist and internationalist, opposing the workers being cannon fodder for bourgeois governments. But within hours of the war starting, almost all socialist parties had backed their own national war efforts. There were exceptions to this, in the Balkans and Russia, and amongst tiny minorities in other countries. But the French Socialists and the German SDP backed the war, even voting for war credits. The revolutionary wing of the movement began to organise itself. In September 1915, following a wave of working-class protests against the war, the Zimmerwald Conference convened in Switzerland, where the left from the Socialist International agreed a position of opposition to the war. In 1916, the Socialist International was dissolved and in 1919, the Third, or Communist, International was formed.

In this context it was hardly surprising that when a new anti-war organisation came into being in September 2001, the Stop the War Coalition (STWC) founders sprang from a range of left traditions, some from far or ultra-left groups. CND nationally did not join STWC, as the membership and support for CND was socially and politically far broader than the framework in which STWC was founded. But CND worked closely in alliance with it to oppose the war and occupation of Iraq and the wars on Afghanistan and Libya. STWC very rapidly won massive and broad support and concerns by some CND members that the left-wing leadership of STWC would take extreme positions that would alienate its broad support turned out to be unfounded. CND and the STWC have also worked with Muslim community organisations, primarily in the early years with the Muslim Association of Britain and subsequently with the British Muslim Initiative. This triple alliance, in which each organisation has unique mobilising capacities, together organised the largest ever demonstration in Britain, of around two million, against the war on Iraq on 15 February 2003.

One of the remarkable features of the anti-war movement had been its continued unity of purpose – ten years on it has not been divided, in spite of the different traditions from which its components hail. What has interested me particularly, in my experience as an officer of the STWC for most of that time, is how the political components that have come together in many of the new European left parties – the realigning post-1989 of the left – have actually come together in a similar way in the STWC. It has been an interesting and very positive experience for me, as a communist, to work in an officers' group – which has met virtually every Friday at 8.30am for the last ten years – which includes not only other communists, but also left Labour, Cliffites, and Trotskyists of various backgrounds. Together we have always been more than the sum of our parts, and a commitment to the shared values of universal human emancipation has generally enabled us to overcome sectarian interests. It is to be hoped that we will maintain this unity when differences of analysis arise, as they have done recently over the war in Libya and protests again the Syrian government.

But of course there is more to being a communist than being anti-war. The chief struggle in Britain, as I write this chapter, is against the cuts imposed by the Tory-led coalition government. Whilst mainstream economists can clearly articulate the alternative to the cuts agenda and argue persuasively for an investment, growth-led recovery, the Labour Party leadership seems as yet unable to respond adequately to the onslaught on working people's living standards, which has nothing to do with economic necessity and everything to do with finishing the work started by Thatcher, of smashing the welfare state and a full introduction of the free market on every level. As a result of her attacks on the trade unions – the organised working class – in the 1980s, the class is weakened, and although there is an increase in working-class militancy which has seen the largest trade union mobilization ever in March 2011, there is as yet no sustained and coordinated opposition to the government agenda from the labour movement to build a hegemonic anti-cuts position in a society where the vast majority are negatively affected by them. This is where in decades past the Communist Party would have played a key role – leading from the left and bringing some measure of unity to the Labour left and trade unions, clearly articulating a people's alternative. The unity of the left achieved in the STWC has not yet been redeveloped for the anti-cuts movement, not least because the natural leaders of such an initiative are the trade unions which organise workers in economic struggle. Small wonder that the absence of a communist party with that political weight, that anchor to the left of the mainstream of the movement, is such a blow to our society. But for those of us that feel its loss, and who want nothing more than to fight for the class, and for the advance of all humanity, there can be no better words than those of the US working class activist Joe Hill: 'Don't mourn – organize!'

No future without Marx

Alistair Findlay

There have been many kinds of marxisms, marxists and interpretations of Marx, including and up to the Marx of the 'post-modernist' philosopher Jacques Derrida, who, rather like Marx, declared himself 'not a Marxist'. If the political history of the twentieth century was indeed 'a dialogue with Marxism', then this dialogue continued despite the collapse of Gorbachev's Soviet Union and the dissolution of the CPGB and other communist parties. Accordingly, in *Specters of Marx* (note the American spelling), the French philosopher of deconstruction (who since 1972 had been a routine visiting professor to Yale and John Hopkins universities) shocked his academic American and French neoliberal followers by denouncing as cold-war rhetoric the political theorist Francis Fukuyama's panegyric on the fall of Soviet communism *The End of History and the Last Man*. 'The Last Man in Europe' was of course the working title of George Orwell's novel *Nineteen Eighty-four*, another text which American cold-war ideologues effectively spun as a critique of Stalinism, though Orwell based most of it on his own and his wife's experiences of working for the government-restricted information service that was the BBC during the Second World War. Far from the collapse of the Berlin Wall signifying the final triumph of liberal democratic capitalism over all other ideologies, as Fukuyama claimed, Derrida proposed that it was only the end of 'a certain concept of history' – Fukuyama's sort, the sterile cultural certainties of the Cold War.

SPECTRES OF MARX

For Derrida, Marx could not simply be 'edited out' of our cultural history. Communism would resist expulsion from Western consciousness — rather as the ghost in *Hamlet* continues to haunt the whole play. The 'spectre of communism' inherent in Marx's thought requires us to reread the *Communist Manifesto's* trenchant critique of liberal democracy 'in the spirit of Marx'. Disclaiming himself a Marxist, Derrida insists that Marx nonetheless remains a cultural figure of considerable consequence, able to speak to us very directly today:

> It will always be a fault not to read and reread and discuss Marx — which is to say also a few others — and to go beyond scholarly 'reading' or 'discussion'. It will be more and more a fault, a failing of theoretical, philosophical, political responsibility. When the dogma machine of the 'Marxist' ideological apparatuses (States, parties, cells, unions, and other places of doctrinal production) are in the process of disappearing, we no longer have any excuse, only alibis, for turning away from this responsibility. There will be no future without this. Not without Marx, no future without Marx, without the memory and the inheritance of Marx: in any case of a certain Marx, of his genius, of at least one of his spirits.

While the plural 'spirits' in that passage may offend some of those reared in the classic tradition of marxism, Derrida's 'insistence on the spirit rather than the letter of Marx's cultural critique' keeps faith with the original, self-critical spirit of Marxism, as he contrasts Fukuyama's defence of the 'ideal' of liberal democracy with its 'real' accompaniments — mass unemployment, the plight of the homeless, the machinations of the arms industry, the manipulation of the United Nations:

> For it must be cried out, at a time when some have the audacity to neo-evangelize in the name of the ideal of a liberal democracy that has finally realized itself as the ideal of human history: never have violence, inequality, exclusion, famine, and thus economic oppression affected as many human beings in the history of the earth and of humanity.

There can be 'no future without Marx', says Derrida — the foremost post-modern critic of 'totalising' ideologies (which include the emancipatory ones such as marxism and feminism, against which the neolibertarian radicals of the 1970s turned their critical firepower just at the moment when the Women's Liberation and European workers' movements were beginning to find some measure of popular support and political traction). Denying that 'deconstruction' was either a 'philosophy' or a 'method', Derrida gave exemplary 'readings' of classic Western philosophic texts (for example Plato, Rousseau) which demonstrated their own limits, gaps and inconsistencies – 'contradictions' – by applying to them their own inner logic. Sound familiar? Marx's 'reading' of Victorian laissez-faire capitalism – *Das Kapital* – applied the logic of bourgeois economists like Adam Smith and Ricardo to demonstrate that it was also creating the seeds of it own destruction, its own nemesis, its own 'gravedigger' (see *Hamlet*), its own contradiction – a propertyless working-class, the proletariat. In a sense, Marx was the first deconstructionist, certainly of capitalism, and from his first reading of that we have had countless 'readings' of Marx ever since.

Suddenly, as Derrida's intervention shows, now that Soviet state communism had fallen, now that the European socialist movement was flat on its back, now that globalisation and international finance capital were in their own estimate 'masters of the universe', Marx 'comes back', at least 'intellectually', a 'revenant' at the feast of global capitalism. Suddenly, a couple of decades further on, it is noticed that the heavy manufacturing industries that Mrs Thatcher buried in Britain, along with the trade union movement they nurtured, were re-appearing in 'third-world' countries; that 'tin-bashing' had eventually created powerful productive economies in Japan, Korea, India, and China (and work forces commensurate with such industries – who perhaps have not spoken yet?), while Britain under Blair and Brown spawned call-centres, supermarkets, financial services, armaments and a housing bubble – all on the 'never never'. How did we get to here?

BACK TO THE FUTURE

My affair with Marxism has entered its fourth decade now, and shows little sign of letting up. We first met in the late 1960s in a watering-hole in Bathgate, the Fairway Hotel, where my older brother Alan and his friends would meet to drink and set the world straight on Thursday evenings, after teaching adult education classes: John Durkin, a professor of history, Bill Drysdale, a principal teacher of English – both old marxists who had befriended the poet and novelist George MacKay Brown via Edwin Muir's Newbattle College in the 1950s – and Eric Atkinson, CPGB organiser for West Lothian. My brother, who was taught politics at Strathclyde University by John Foster, would dissect the developing AES (Alternative Economic Strategy), Bill burst into Shelley, John championed the sans-culottes, Eric the latest strike at the local Leyland tractor factory, and my father, a former miner turned editor of the local district newspaper, would bravely defend the Wilson government before falling back on Burns. I laughed and listened.

It was no surprise to me, therefore, in 1971-3 to hear Mick McGahey and Jimmy Reid's brilliant oratory at mass public demos – eloquent, funny, pugnacious, intelligent, unkind to Tory governments. To me this was simply the public face of Scottish marxism, no menacing reds under the beds, just working-class autodidacts, informed, combative, no prisoners taken. At college studying for social work, Marx came wrapped academically in sociology lectures. I would later read Stuart Hall on working-class youth cultures, *Resistance Through Rituals* and *Policing the Crisis*, and similar stuff such as Paul Willis's *Learning to Labour* (published by the Birmingham Centre for Contemporary Culture). The Centre had been founded by the Leavisite literary critic, Richard Hoggart, but was then developed in a New Left cultural studies direction by Hall utilising Althusserian and Gramscian marxism. I found these texts relevant to my perspectives as a professional social worker. I also read the marxist critique of the welfare state when I undertook an MA in Social Studies at Bradford University in the late 1970s – including the radical framework suggested by Peter Leonard, the social history of hooligans and moral panics by Geoff Pearson, and the feminist-marxist critique of women and welfare by writers like Elizabeth Wilson and Bea Campbell. While I was in England, Mrs Thatcher appeared. I left.

When I returned to Edinburgh in 1980, I became active in the white-collar union, NALGO, as did other social workers, many responding for the first time politically to Mrs Thatcher's attack on local government jobs and services. I joined the CPGB in April 1982 – the folksinger Dick Gaughan enrolled me – when Michael Foot committed Her Majesty's Loyal Opposition to supporting Mrs Thatcher in sending a Task Force to the Falklands, in the teeth of American disapproval and while she was the most unpopular prime minister on record. The ensuing war killed 257 British servicemen, 3 islanders and 649 Argentinian conscripts for the sake of a small colony of British ex-pats (sheep-shaggers in blazers), who could have been resettled on a small Scottish island in the Hebrides for an ounce of the cost and with no loss of life. Instead, Mrs T's war got Mrs T re-elected the following year by a landslide, except in Scotland.

When I joined the CPGB, I did not do so seeking 'comradeship' or 'a way of life', far less political 'power' or to fulfil a radical family political tradition. I had a busy enough life, thank you very much, working and studying and playing football, and I knew the personal burden that political and trade union activism placed on my socialist friends in the Labour Party, never mind the hyper-active CP. I joined because I saw Mrs Thatcher for the class threat I thought she was, not to a socialist Scotland (such a thing remained even then a dream), but to social democratic Scotland, where the welfare state was viewed as an unquestioned 'good', providing quality public housing, quality public education and quality public health and welfare services – which needed improvement, certainly, but now required defending against a Tory onslaught involving cut-back, privatisation and sell-off.

When I joined the CPGB in Edinburgh it was already split between 'Euros' and 'Traditionalists' – or 'Tankies', the more frequently used pejorative term. I thus met 'The Kalashnikov Brothers', to whom that term was perhaps not entirely inappropriate, a pair of disputatious eccentrics who 'haunted' the Leith branch. Innocent of the nature and extent of the split, I immediately and inadvertently warmed myself to 'The KB's' by voting for their amendment to a motion at my first branch meeting because, being entirely non-aligned, I judged it the best considered and best argued position. Across Edinburgh as a whole, certainly amongst the leadership, the majority supported the 1978 *British Road to Socialism* line that 'class' was not the only factor making people aware of their exploitation under capitalism. The Leith branch, however, tended to be gathered under the more traditional 'class warrior' banner of the *Morning Star* Supporters Club. Things rubbed along up to and during the miner's strike, 1984-5, but come its 'defeat' (*Marxism Today*) or 'set-back' (*Morning Star*), the membership of both camps began to disappear like snow off the proverbial dyke. By the late 1980s I ended up as acting secretary of the Leith branch, trying to get rid of piles of *Seven Days* that no one seemed prepared to collect, far less distribute. Comrades retreated into their own 'interests' – peace, environment, trade unions, the Campaign for a Scottish Assembly. Edinburgh CPGB simply withered on the vine, became a 'ghost branch', a dead parrot.

I hated the dull slog of branch routine, such as it was, but enjoyed wonderful moments. I never regretted not joining the Labour Party, an electoral vehicle too often dominated by careerists and sand-dancers, in spite of the socialist convictions of many of its activists and supporters, even before the advent of New Labour. I remember Gordon McLennan's thrilled and thrilling report back of his meetings with Gorbachev when he was in London to see Mrs Thatcher. Gordon said from the start that Gorby was the real deal, a genuine moderniser, and it was impossible not to believe his own shining conviction on that score. The internationalist dimension of the CPGB was evident, with speakers from resistance movements from all over the world, and political refugees, coming to and passing through Edinburgh. Going to packed Dick Gaughan concerts during the miner's strike was inspiring and humbling in equal measure. I remember speaking with John Kay, the Scottish Organiser, in a pub at the foot of Leith Walk, asking why Mick McGahey did not 'tell Scargill' to accept MacGregor's offer to include 'social reasons' as a basis for keeping 'uneconomic' pits from closing. It seemed to me then, as it does now, that all the miners needed at that point was 'a draw' against Mrs Thatcher to interrupt her momentum and political ascendancy – which would have been a tremendous result, given the clear determination of the Nottinghamshire miners not to strike without a ballot. John quietly explained that you do not 'tell' major trade union leaders like Scargill anything. I still believe McGahey would have led that strike differently, and much more 'politically' than the ultra-left rhetoric coming out of 'Our Arthur'. The array of issues and movements that dedicated comrades led or participated in – Peace, South Africa, People's March for Jobs, Poll Tax – was by turns hectic, demanding, bewildering and sometimes genuinely uplifting.

During the CPGB's own internal battle, I read both *Marxism Today* and the *Morning Star*, and enjoyed both. I thought they each reached parts that the other could not, and latterly, perhaps, did not want to either. I was perhaps in a minority of one in believing that the party still needed and benefitted from both its trade union core and the networks it was nurturing with metropolitan groups and single issue movements during the period – peace, women, environment, human rights – activities and perspectives not unlike the Popular Front of the 1930s, but extending well beyond parties and onto the terrain of 'the personal is political'. Tolerance and respect ran out amongst both sets of activists and the party folded in circumstances almost as rancorous on the left as they had been on its founding in 1920. I stayed till the end, mainly focused on the Campaign for a Scottish Assembly. For many communists towards the end, the focus of their activity continued to be the trade union or peace or green movements, et cetera, not 'the party' itself. Any 'gap' one may have felt 'after the party' may well have been cushioned by this in many ways traditional aspect of CPGB activism; it was a campaigning organisation rather than an electorally programmed one like the Labour Party.

I realised that the battle had been fought over 'ideas', obviously, but also for 'inclusion', surely, even of its own class-warriors. Kinnock's expulsion of Militant from the Labour Party, a tiny enclave of ultra-lefts amongst an historically revisionist party, was as nothing compared to the blood-letting involved when an ostensibly 'soft left' CPGB executive, while offering 'broad democratic alliances' to non-marxist groups, individuals and parties, flatly proscribed the views of almost 30-40 per cent of its membership. To adapt Nietzsche – regretfully – those who fight dragons too long themselves become dragons. I do not say the leadership was not often provoked, but it certainly provided a terrible example for New Labour to take down from the shelf when Blair, Brown and Mandelson got round to clearing out from the movement, not wild-eyed Militant Trots, but solid, socialist, sitting Labour MPs like Dennis Canavan – who simply stood as an Independent MP to retain his Falkirk seat at Westminster. By articulating the case for 'modernising' socialism through the 1980s and then vacating the field in the 1990s, it strikes me that the CPGB opened the way for New Labour, not to bring forward popular socialism, the CPGB's goal, but for something deeply unreconstructed in Labour's right-wing psyche since the time of Gaitskell and Crosland in the 1950s: the desire to ditch the Labour Party's links with the trade union movement, without which socialism in this country is pretty much unthinkable, not to say unachievable. The trade union movement is not a guarantor of socialism, certainly, but it is an essential one, and still the only countervailing force capable of resisting and defeating capitalism – even more obvious now that national governments no longer exercise control over the bankers unleashed by Blair and Brown. A Labour government, without the backing of the trade union and other popular movements and power bases outside parliament, will remain isolated in parliament; it will be the prisoner of the global corporate capitalist interests which fund capitalist parties, and own the bulk of the popular media, which promotes a public discourse that favours the rich and the few against the interests of the vast majority – as the present Con-Lib coalition is now demonstrating every day it continues.

FLIGHT OF THE PHOENIX

When the CPGB crashed and burned I left Edinburgh in 1991 to return to my native county of West Lothian, all of half-an-hour along the road, and began a period of study, research, writing and introspection entirely untrammelled by active left political in-fighting and argument. During the 1980s I had also been reading another political magazine, a bi-monthly called *Radical Scotland*, which had on its editorial board a couple of CPGB academics, Willie Thompson and John Fairley. This offered a political-cultural forum similar to *Marxism Today*, a place where left Labourites, nationalists, liberals, communists, socialists and anarchists could exchange views, insults, book reviews and the occasional brilliant insight – all in the cause of the Campaign for a Scottish Parliament, though inevitably the anti-Poll Tax Campaign also made use of its pages. The magazine carried cartoons, short stories and occasional poems, which I believed I could improve upon. I set about writing 'Brithers' (about my father, my brothers and socialism – also a world of 'brothers') only to find that, rather like *Marxism Today*, thinking its job done, *Radical Scotland* packed up, its fifty-first and final issue appearing in August 1991. So I sent my poem to the Scots literary magazine, *Cencrastus*, named in honour of Hugh MacDiarmid, which published it alongside an article by Angus Calder on the Nigerian poet Niyi Osundare (whom he compared to Neruda and Brecht), an article by Douglas Dunn on Hugh MacDiarmid, and articles on Sorley MacLean, Robert Garioch and Iain Crichton Smith, a 'flyting' by the Glasgow radical folksinger Adam MacNaughton, and a review of William McIlvanney's latest novel. Hamish Henderson was missing, but would turn up often enough in other issues, as he had done before, both as subject and commentator.

And so I entered my own *New Times*, the world of Scots literature, history and culture – particularly the parts with strongly inflected marxist-socialist-republican-feminist accents, which is quite a lot in fact, and much of the best, arguably – bequeathed by the various 'waves' of the movement that had been kick-started from a back kitchen in 1920s Montrose by Hugh MacDiarmid and called the Scottish Literary Renaissance. Whatever time and energy I had ever given to the party was doubled and trebled from this point on, channelled into Scots poetry, literature and language. I attended week-long Arvon writing courses run by the likes of Tom Leonard, Kathleen Jamie, Liz Lochhead, Jackie Kay and Brendan Kennelly. I took a course in Scottish Cultural Studies and met up with the poet and novelist Robert Alan Jamieson. I took an M.Phil. in Modern Poetry at Stirling University, and had my first book published, *Shale Voices*, a 'creative memoir' cum social history of the shale mining communities of West Lothian, which drew on marxist labour-social history perspectives 'from below'. I might now summarise all of the above by saying that I was a marxist before I joined the CPGB, I was a marxist when it dissolved itself in 1991, and I have been a marxist – certainly *culturally* – ever since.

In the last decade I have published four collections of poetry – *Sex, Death and Football*, *The Love Songs of John Knox*, *Dancing With Big Eunice* and *Never Mind the Captions*, all from Luath Press, a small independent Edinburgh publisher. All of these collections assume and work on the basis that society is divided by class, wealth, religion and gender, and the cultures arising therefrom. All contain poems which refer to marxism or marxists, often by introducing or exploring a 'popular voice' within the 'high cultural' arena of 'poetry'. This was certainly in my mind when compiling and editing an anthology of football poetry, *100 Favourite Scottish Football Poems*, which contains poems by many of modern Scotland's most accomplished poets – MacDiarmid, Morgan, Lochhead, Leonard, Dunn, Kay – waxing lyrical about Scotland's most popular, if not necessarily its most successful, pastime (apart perhaps from golf or, indeed, bowls).

My most directly marxist work concerns an anthology of 'the poetry of Scottish Marxism' – *Lenin's Gramophone* – which I have been compiling and thinking about on and off over the last ten years, and which still awaits completion. The title comes from the famous criticism John MacLean made of William Gallacher during their dispute in 1920 over whether to take the Scottish marxist left into a British-wide communist party or a Scottish based one, a dispute Gallacher 'won' at the cost of MacLean calling him 'the gramophone of Lenin'. This was not the worst thing to be called on Red Clydeside, of course, during the Bolshevik Revolution when Lenin's reputation was at its zenith. The point the title wishes to underline is the fault-line that has run through Scottish marxism ever since, most notably represented within Scottish cultural marxism by the arguments between the professedly Leninist Hugh MacDiarmid and the Gramscian inspired poet, balladeer and oral cultural excavator and archivist, and genius of the School of Scottish Studies, Hamish Henderson. Just as MacLean and Gallacher were Bolsheviks who took different views on the national question, MacDiarmid and Henderson – Leninist and Gramscian marxists respectively – agree on the national question. How to account for, deal with, such plural paradox?

Laying aside the exact details of the disagreements between all these major figures of Scottish marxism, political and literary, such differences seem to me to emphasise what is most obvious about marxism in general, and Scottish marxism in particular: not its monolithic nature, but its fluidity, length and breadth. Scottish marxists, including the vast range of Scottish poets, writers and artists who, at one time or another, considered themselves 'marxist', often held divergent views on various topics, split into different parties, or none, have been academics or welders, and have ranged historically from physical force Chartists to Poll-Tax Campaigners and tree-hugging Eurocommunists. *Lenin's Gramophone* sets out to reflect this, to be an inclusive anthology, one capable of demonstrating and tracing the long roots of British marxism through the poetry that its various adherents wrote, claimed or spawned – often under the international influence of American democratic republicans like Walt Whitman in the nineteenth century, and the militant socialist poetry of Carl Sandburg, as well as Soviet and European radical writers and artists like Mayakovsky, Brecht, Neruda and Hikmet through the twentieth century. As William Gallacher famously said at some point in the 1930s, probably during the CPGB's turn away from the sectarian 'class against class' period to the 'popular front' policy of collaborating with social democratic forces in order to defeat fascism and thereby protect the 'workers' state', the Soviet Union: 'we are a movement, not a monument'. Compiling the literary products of that movement's origins in the nineteenth century and subsequent development in Scotland through the poetry of predominantly Scottish marxist poets, writers, critics and historians is the task I set myself with *Lenin's Gramophone*.

Taking this insight and applying it to the circumstances of modern Scottish writers from the 1920s on, but extrapolating beyond marxist writers to include socialists and left nationalists as well, suggested to me that the several 'waves' of the Scottish Literary Renaissance might usefully be viewed as having operated like a series of 'popular cultural fronts' – writers consciously opposed to 'kailyard literature' – though not all of these writers were necessarily in agreement as to what kind of literature-politics should replace this, apart from that it should be something decidedly to the left of the prevailing status quo. A literary-cultural movement developed, the Scottish Literary Renaissance, a left modernist movement of poets, writers and artists, brought together not through adherence to the CPGB, far less 'Moscow', but in writing 'against' the existing establishment, literary and political. They were an otherwise motley crew of political marxists, socialists, republicans and left nationalists. The first wave of this 'cultural front' was arguably led/inspired from the 1920s to the 1950s by agendas and examples set by Hugh MacDiarmid; the second wave, up to the 1960s to the 1970s, was influenced similarly by Hamish Henderson; and a third wave, through the 1980s to the 1990s, was hallmarked and given experimental substance across a wide range of genres and styles by the likes of Tom Leonard and Edwin Morgan who, like MacDiarmid and Henderson, was a Scottish republican. Arguably, a fourth wave is discernable, comprising feminist-women poets who followed in the wake of Liz Lochhead from the 1970s, a breakthrough which has since been acknowledged and 'completed' by Lochhead's recently having been made Scotland's 'Makar', following the death of Edwin Morgan, and the appointment last year of Carol Ann Duffy as the first female, the first bisexual, the first Scots and the first socialist British Poet Laureate.

The Scottish Literary Renaissance was not, as its name may imply, merely a 'literary' movement, but one that was bound up with issues to do with political sovereignty, and all that that meant in terms of social and cultural expression, language, nationhood and identity. It was a movement of artists and writers – not of political alignment, though it was broadly left – who wished to explore and express the contemporaneity of Scotland, the modern, against the kilted imagery imposed on the popular imagination by the novels of Sir Walter Scott and the rural, peasant community addressed by Burns. This tradition has since turned 'Kailyard', becoming diluted and hackneyed by conservative and religious novelists like Ian MacLaren, Samuel Crockett, J.M. Barrie and John Buchan (a Tory politician who became Governor General of Canada between the wars). Such writers ignored the industrialisation of nineteenth-century Scotland and its class-divided reality, producing instead a narrative depicting harmonious hamlets in wee glens, brig o' doon film-sets and derring-do heroes settling the

Empire and taking-on Johnny Foreigner. This narrative continued almost unabated through to the 1960s in Scotland's most popular weekly newspaper, *The Sunday Post*, published by the right-wing D.C. Thomson group based in Dundee, whose 'The Broons' and 'Oor Wullie', kitch cartoons of Scottish life and sentiment, are perhaps its most remarkable ideological invention. Its role in maintaining and reflecting Scotland's public cultural backwardness prompted Tom Nairn to declare in the 1970s that Scotland would never be free 'until the last Kirk minister is strangled by the last copy of *The Sunday Post*'.

For the purposes of my projected anthology, the Scottish Literary Renaissance is broken into three 'waves', each period marked by major shifts in the marxist thought and politics within the CPGB and the breakaway New Left. The early Bolshevism of the 1920s that was replaced by the Popular Front politics of the 1930s and the Second War, dominated poetically and critically by MacDiarmid, are designated as the first period; the Cold War and de-colonisation occurring through the 1950s and 1960s saw the rise of Edinburgh People's Cultural Festivals and a folk movement opposed to nuclear weapons initiated by Hamish Henderson, who became part of the New Left – this was a period when marxism would become both more intellectual-cultural and less reliant on 'party' (meaning the CPGB and the Labour Party left); the late 1960s-1970s saw the rise of the women's movement and the turn towards Eurocommunism by the CPGB, culminating in its 1978 rewriting of *The British Road to Socialism*, which advocated broad democratic alliances with social democratic parties, single-issue and human rights groups and movements in order to defeat and outflank right-wing Tory policies. These forces would indeed come together in the 1980s-1990s in campaigns such as Greenham Common, the anti-poll tax movement, and the Campaign for a Scottish Assembly – protests not restricted to card-carrying Marxists and barred to no one except card-carrying Thatcherites. This brief outline may thus serve to convey the nature and extent of my background and interest in what I have termed 'cultural Marxism' and its application to Scottish literature and culture. I would now like to broach more immediate and contemporary matters.

DEAD PARROTS – SITTING DUCKS

By the late 1980s Mrs Thatcher's political project was stalled by a broad democratic coalition opposed to the Poll Tax, only to be supplanted in the 1990s by what she considered her greatest political achievement: New Labour. There is not a little irony in the fact that while Blair and Brown were off trying to woo 'middle-England' voters, Alex Salmond's SNP Party, then government, proceeded to steal from beneath their noses the wide constituency that still exists in Scotland for public sector economics, and universal welfare benefits – including free public education, which has always appealed to Scottish middle-class and working-class voters alike. The irony resides in two facts: the SNP remained outwith the cross-party movement which actually achieved a devolved Scottish Parliament in 1999, and which has since brought the SNP back from 'the dead' to which New Labour had hoped such a limited parliament might consign it; and the current SNP majority government (a thing once thought impossible to achieve by its Labourist architects) demolished New Labour at the 2011 Scottish Parliamentary election, along with the Lib Dems and the Tories, on the relatively mild political prospectus of defending the health service, free university fees, free home care for the elderly plus bus travel. There is now no Scottish Labour politician who can claim a political platform to the left of Alex Salmond, and none with the debating skills to outwit him in the Scottish Parliament. Tommy Sheridan and the handful of Scottish Socialist MSPs – whom he led well enough for the first few years of the Parliament – have been blasted out of the water on the back of a lurid sex scandal involving the *News of the World* and a court case that would have done harm to the reputation of Rab C. Nesbitt.

And yet we are living through the most astonishing political and economic upheaval since the 1930s! No one knows where the current banking crisis will end up. There is a minority Tory Government being supported in Westminster on a daily basis by a renegade Lib Dem consortium which has already been demolished at the polls in Scotland. The Scottish Labour Party is now to have a leader separate from the UK leader, with a list of contenders unknown to the Scottish electorate and already being sized up by Alex Salmond, licking his sizeable chops. Jim Murphy, a rising star in Labour's Shadow Cabinet, has already refused to consider taking on Salmond by becoming the leader of Scottish Labour in the Scots Parliament – and who could blame him?

Salmond's strategy seems clear enough. He has demonstrated the SNP's capacity to 'govern Scotland', as a minority government at least as well as New Labour during its several years in office, and he is now 'standing up for Scotland's interests' against an unpopular, and unelected, Con-Lib Coalition government in Westminster, unloved by the populace at large and also by each coalition party's right and left wings. (Cameron-Clegg seem prepared to split their parties at the next election, thus forming a centre-right party divested of their own respective problematic 'wings' – the Europhobes and the Libertarians.) Salmond is currently hoping to delay the holding of a Referendum in Scotland on additional powers for the Scottish Parliament up to and including more financial powers (Devolution Min) through federalism (Devolution Max) to Independence (Separatism, whatever that means) – all against the background of his government in Edinburgh defending Scottish interests against a cost-cutting Con-Lib Coalition which the Scottish electorate did not, and will not, vote for. Scotland is unlikely to vote for separatism, but by the time that the referendum is held it might well go as far as federalism, depending on the economic-political position – and whether or not Alex Salmond has gone under a proverbial bus.

That such cataclysmic political changes seem not only feasible but imminent is surely a lesson to marxists of my generation, especially those still active directly politically, as I have not been for years. I see my own contribution as residing in the cultural sphere as described above, writing, speaking, occasionally marching and demonstrating, but not joining a political party. I have recently been invited to give talks at *Morning Star* events on the theme of 'our culture: our class', and that seems to me to be where my best abilities and interest lie. As the current political scene unfolds I see increasing parallels with the need in the 1980s-90s for the political right to be outflanked by a broad democratic front – similar to what did for Mrs Thatcher – and spearheaded by an aroused trade union movement. In Scotland, I think federalism would be the best destination for the left to pursue, with Scotland raising its own revenue and 'buying-in' to Westminster in terms of a defence and foreign policy which 'we', the Scottish people, would agree to. In these terms, Scotland would not in my view have gone to war in the Falklands, Afghanistan or Iraq, though quite possibly it would have helped in Kosovo, given the humanitarian issues involved.

RETURN OF THE REPRESSED

The CPGB dissolved itself, and yet the class struggle did not disappear, just as its minority 'wing', the CPB, did not disappear either, nor the *Morning Star*. Both are still 'there', and we ought to acknowledge this and respect that, if we remain any kind of socialist at all. I was recently interested to learn that Alasdair Gray, the veteran Scottish painter and novelist, has always read the *Morning Star*, and still does, to find out 'what real workers think'. Whenever I want to find out what Scottish marxism thinks politically and analytically I am always pleased to read John Foster. I therefore cite this extract from his contribution to *Is there a Scottish Road to Socialism?*, written some four years ago, prior to the banking crisis which has since beset global capitalism. Foster is describing what he terms the 'political' vulnerability of British state monopoly capitalism; he insists – almost 'counter-intuitively' given the complete hold that global capitalist interests had on the policies of the New Labour government at the time – that the British state is in fact 'far weaker today – both politically and economically – than in the 1970s'. If this was at all accurate four years ago, then how much more accurate must such an assessment be today in the wake of the still unfolding crisis we are currently witnessing:

> British state monopoly capitalism would immediately be placed on the defensive by a very moderate set of demands – no more than a partial return to the pre-1979 situation in terms of a reversal of failed privatizations in transport, energy, pensions and housing and an end to the nuclear military alliance with the United States. Today such demands are both economically necessary for the developmental regeneration of the British economy and politically supported by a

majority within the population – at the same time as neo-liberal policies have largely lost credibility. Today, neither the Conservative Party nor 'new' Labour are easily able to deliver the new tranche of reforms on the public sector (further privatization in education and health), the labour market (forcing more people into the bottom end of the jobs market) or pensions (cutting the entitlements of those in both the public and private sectors) deemed essential to maintain monopoly profits. 'New' Labour, despite being manufactured as the chosen vehicle for neo-liberal politics, has lost its ability to control the trade union movement and increasingly the Labour Party itself. Elsewhere in Europe, in France and Germany particularly, there is a parallel inability of monopoly capital to manage mass politics on its own terms – though here in circumstances where the working class has retained many more of its post-war gains and where the battle starts at a higher ground.

'No future without Marx', said Derrida, two decades ago, and I for one believe him. It would of course be easy to become over-sentimental about the heroic struggles and figures of 'the past', of the CPGB being able to conjure up the kind of broad democratic front campaigns and alliances that helped defeat Thatcher and the Poll Tax. Yet all's to do again – as the poet said. And why not? That remains, as it always was, the challenge facing us today. And since I am a poet, I would like to close this article by invoking some of that old staunchness which the CPGB personified at its best in figures like Michael McGahey about whom I wrote the following poem – 'Michael McGahey's Portrait by Maggie Hambling' – which appeared in a tribute to the Scottish radical historian, scholar and poet, Angus Calder, entitled *For Angus*:

> Not for you full Highland regalia,
> Clan Chief sporran, kilted monarch of the Glen,
> garb of some Public Schoolboy Robber Baron,
> capital sunk in South African diamond mines, off-shore
> scams, grouse-moors, the whole Victoriana pantomime.
> You sit four-square, National Health specs not there,
> but still, you wear the respectable suit of your class –
> worn too by Lenin, and John MacLean, your father's

red blood coursing through your veins, for he too was
an aristocrat – of Labour, a foundation member of the British
Communist Party – who thought you a compromiser, and
you agreed, for so too was Gallacher, who said: 'we are
a movement, not a monument'. You led with your head,
a marvellous orator, steeped in literature, gravel-voiced,
whose aim was a republic, here, in this place, built,
as you were, on brains, commonsense, and laughter.

McGahey's portrait hangs in the National Portrait Gallery of Scotland in Edinburgh, surrounded by images of monarchy and the ancient Scottish ruling class in their togs – imperious, kilted, senatorial – set against backgrounds of moor and mountain, an iconography that 'the common man' attire worn by generations of Mick's class strove to assign to the dustbin of history. What remains is to divest that still privileged remnant not just of its 'breeks', but of its power, and with that to create a better society, a more inclusive culture, one that is international and outward-looking – everything that the CPGB represented in the Scottish context in figures like McGahey, Reid and Airley.

Towards a marxist theory of love; *or* the personal is post-political

Andrew Pearmain

THESIS

I joined the Communist Party in the summer of 1975. I was just turning twenty-one and back at my mother's house in Leeds for the summer vacation, between first and second years of my philosophy degree at Manchester University. I don't really remember why I joined, other than a vague feeling that I ought to get involved in something political. With my family background and the mood of the times it would have to be left-wing. I'd seen enough of the Labour Party in South Leeds to put me off for life (though I would later spend six dispiriting years in it, either side of the millennium). We'd get an election leaflet every four or five years in this 'rock-solid' but visibly crumbling constituency, and very little in between bar the odd speech or ceremonial opening by the MP (Hugh Gaitskell when I was a child, then Merlyn Rees). I was practical enough to know that the assorted Trots and anarchists I'd seen running around the university were not serious options. When a CP leaflet came through my mother's door, with the craggy face of Bert Ramelson (local parliamentary candidate and renowned national CP industrial organiser), I filled it in and sent it off – yes, I would like to join the struggle for a Socialist Britain.

A few weeks later a small, freckled and furtive ginger-haired man came round to see me at my mum's. My details had found their way to King Street then back to him, the secretary of the local branch. Even then I got the impression that this, a response to a random leaflet, was not a common form of recruitment. Over the years the

CP must have distributed millions of them, but it was probably more about keeping existing members busy than bringing in new ones. We sat in my mother's front room, all too aware of her in the kitchen down the hall, and discussed the 'policies and perspectives' of what from then on was always called 'the party'. I asked him 'What about Russia?' and he replied, a little ruefully, 'Well, we're a lot more critical than we used to be.' I attended a local branch meeting – an odd collection of people I'd never otherwise seen around the neighbourhood – in the scruffy attic of a terraced house. I found the atmosphere of tetchy intrigue, even during mundane discussions of minutes and fundraising, by turns alluring and off-putting. There were glimpses of unspoken enmities and associations, but at that stage I had no idea what they were about. This was both a secret and an open society, full of contradictions and undercurrents, not too dissimilar from the Catholic parish I'd been brought up in. At the same time these were serious subversives. My God, communists! Me, lonely and shy, with far too much of my time spent alone with my records and books and lonely young man's thoughts and feelings, now one amongst them. In the same room!

I had recently taken up with a new girlfriend. I told her all about 'the Party', and relished her fear and fascination. I tried half-heartedly to recruit her, because I thought I was supposed to, but for the moment she was happy to let me get on with it. She did tell her parents, enjoyed their scandalised reaction, and gleefully recounted it to me as we sat holding hands in the pub. Between snogs and slurps of beer, I'd be explaining that the Social Contract was in fact a social con-trick, that the EEC was not all it was cracked up to be, and that under socialism everybody would have sex whenever they wanted (unlike us there and then; she was holding out till at least our second month). It was an odd relationship. She was several years younger than me, and still at school. The sister of an old school friend of mine, I now think I went out with her as a way of keeping close to him. The 'sixties' never really arrived in Leeds. Same-sex crushes had to be kept at a fastidious distance, with in this case a compliant girl in between. Whatever, a pattern was being established here, of my youthful political affiliations and personal relationships getting inextricably, often messily and destructively, tangled up.

I went back to university in Manchester, threw myself into student activism and the hectic social and political life of one of the largest and liveliest CP student branches in the country, and rather struggled to keep up my inter-city relationship with my friend's sister back in Leeds. I remember weekend visits by her to Manchester and me back to Leeds, letters and postcards warily pledging undying love, lots of awkward silences with her among my new student comrades (who must have seemed like Martians to this Catholic grammar schoolgirl), and eventually quite good sex in my dingy bedsit or her room when her parents were at Sunday mass. We split up abruptly in the Christmas vacation back in Leeds, and I spent several days crying in my room at my mother's house; more at the indignity of being dumped, I suspect, than from deep hurt at the loss of this particular girlfriend. It did leave me bruised and wary, and for all the hurly burly and plentiful sexual opportunity of communist student life, I kept myself to myself for most of the following year, 1976, into my third and final academic year.

By this stage I was well established in the party branch, and on my way to an elected sabbatical position in the students union (quite an achievement, in between strong Tory and ultra left contingents). The new academic year had brought a crop of new comrades, among them a genuinely new recruit, a tall and very attractive first-year sociology student called Helen. Unlike me, she'd done some shopping around before joining the CP, even attending other groups' meetings before deciding they weren't for her. She told me later that she spent over a year trying to join the Labour Party at home in Wiltshire, but either they weren't interested in young people, or like other rotten boroughs elsewhere they were 'full'. Helen was beautiful, in an unaffected unadorned way probably better described as 'handsome'. She wore jeans and shirts and jumpers, and sensible shoes and coats; very rarely dresses or make-up. I remember the shock on the few occasions she did, a functional flowery skirt and two quick strokes of lipstick. It had me lusting hard after her, and disturbed by my own desire. Helen was an ardent feminist, but she was also securely heterosexual. Once I urged her into bed with another woman, the girlfriend of a fellow student union official (a really nice Tory by the way), who had just been diagnosed with cancer (he died a few months later, and left me to fight the Trots and anarchists on my own). I think she did it out of public-spiritedness – she had lots of that, which used to slightly mystify our comrades – and to placate me rather than her 'inner lesbian'.

For all our political bravado and outward social confidence, neither Helen nor I were very good at love. We had both had plenty of girlfriends and boyfriends (the manager of a soon-to-be-famous pop group on her side), but neither of us had learnt or benefitted much from any of them. I think we kind of fell into each other in quiet, lonely desperation; we were both communists, and we probably thought that was enough. We were very different people, from very different social circumstances and parts of the country. But we were quite similar personality-types, what I would later hear described as 'gregarious loners', competent in company, needing occasional bursts of it, but actually more comfortable on our own. Our best times together were usually spent in silence, studying or reading, watching films or TV, walking or travelling. Things only got complicated when we talked too much, so we tended not to.

After a while I moved in with Helen in one of the notorious Hulme crescents. They were built in the 1960s (or rather thrown together, so it all slowly came apart), populated with students and pensioners in the 1970s, emptied of legitimate tenants by the late 1980s, and finally demolished in the 1990s and replaced with the kind of terraced rows they had originally replaced. It was great for students, handy for the university and beyond it the city, and seriously low-rent. The Aaben cinema was just round the corner; we saw every incomprehensible foreign film we could. The Factory was just beyond that; I went a few times on my own, to see bands never since heard of. My clearest memories of my time with Helen are of the summer of 1977: sunbathing on her mossy balcony, a glorious week together at the Communist University of London, two more weeks of 'Eurocommunism' in Italy, where we slept at a friend's flat in Genova and had sticky sex on cushions on his marble floor, then in a proper bed in a *pensione* in Florence.

We didn't know it at the time, but this was a kind of heyday for us and for the party. That year's CPGB Congress endorsed the 'revised' *British Road to Socialism*, the party programme first drafted at Stalin's instigation in 1950. The 1977 *BRS* retained a surprising amount of the old formulations, but incorporated enough of the new, more open and democratic 'Eurocommunism' to make us feel things were moving rapidly in our direction. The Congress proceedings were even filmed for television, and broadcast in a prime-time Granada TV documentary *Decision: British Communism*, which we all watched shouting out and pointing at people we knew. The 1977 CUL was vibrant, almost triumphalist: over 1000 communists and fellow travellers gathered at the University of London Union in Malet Street endlessly talking and laughing, swapping Gramsci quotes alongside punk lyrics, and thinking up ways to unsettle our more straight-laced fellow comrades back in the real world of the 'wages struggle' and public spending cuts. We got high on the broad democratic alliance. For a brief moment, being communist was cool.

I don't really know what happened with me and Helen. Well, maybe I do. I started sleeping with other women on my trips to London, other communist students and even a Tory member of the NUS Executive (whose taste for rough sex really shocked me; she later joined the SDP). I know now that it was wrong, but by the confused personal morality of the time I thought it might not be. Besides it was more often something that happened to me than something I engineered (yes I know, 'typical man', but this is what much of my young life felt like). What would normally happen is that after a day's meeting we would all retire to the pub or a restaurant, then back to somebody's house to smoke dope or (later) snort cocaine (yes, commies took drugs). Eventually I would find myself alone with a woman, who would take me to her bed and attempt to have sex with me, not generally satisfactorily because we were both by then too stoned or tired. We would wake up the next morning, predictably sheepish and embarrassed, and act like nothing had happened. Which, quite often, hadn't. But it happened often enough to undermine my relationship with Helen, and make going back to her in Manchester seem like a retreat.

There is a theory, supported by supposedly scientific research, that the natural lifespan of a sexual relationship is two years. Over that period some chemical builds up and then falls away. More simply we get bored with each other, and fall out of love. All I know is that my relationship with Helen was my fullest and most long-lasting up to then, at pretty exactly two years, and that over the next year I went looking for a way out. I found it firstly in postgraduate study at Leicester University, my first stab at Gramscian research under the aristocratic communist educationalist Brian Simon – a lovely man but a hopeless supervisor. By the end of my first year (with several token trips back to Helen in Manchester, including the momentous general election night of 1979, when we held each other tight and tearfully pledged 'not to let our dreams die') I realised my research wasn't really going anywhere. I let myself get sidetracked back into student politics, briefly in the students union at Leicester but soon afterwards as a 'part-timer' on the NUS executive. This required pretty much permanent residence in London, claiming the dole but working harder than I've ever done before or since. After several months of sleeping on comrades' floors and sofas (and if I was welcome, beds), I made one last trip back to Manchester to tell Helen it was over. She'd already reached that conclusion herself, but I felt awful about it. It was supposed to be amicable, comradely even, but I never saw or heard from her again. I heard from someone else that she moved to Scotland and a not wholly satisfactory marriage, with a couple of kids, but I know no more. I would expect her not to like me very much.

ANTITHESIS

My first sight of Nicky was in the corridors of the Imperial Hotel in wet and cold Blackpool in December 1979, at my first NUS Conference as an executive member. I had already heard of this bright young woman just out of school who had taken charge of the small CP student branch at Newcastle University (a rather sedate bunch of scientists and postgraduates), made it (goodness me!) trendy and started recruiting other 'real students', not just people born into the party or losers and misfits who simply didn't belong anywhere else. She was small and wiry, like a coiled spring, with a slight squint and granny glasses, and a dress sense several notches up the feminist gauge from Helen's: an old army greatcoat, dirty torn jeans and huge scuffed Dr Marten boots. She had a voracious appetite for drugs, and a capacity to remain functional throughout that amazed me. I'd take a toke off a morning spliff and go back to sleep, while she'd roar off out for another day of world-shattering. For a while we slept together chastely, end-of-the-night shared-sofa stuff, but when she discovered I'd had sex with someone else in the Camden squat I was living in, she seemed to decide we should too. The thing about Nicky, which I kind of knew at the time but kind of chose to disregard, was that she really was a lesbian, sexually as well as 'politically' (this latter meant feminists who had sex with women but didn't really like it, so still had sex with men but didn't really like *them*). I should have known from Nicky's previous sexual history (what little there was of it), as well as the perfunctory doped-out sex we usually ended up having, that I was an aberration. This might have warned me off, or at least made it easier to bear what happened later. But I'm getting ahead of myself.

By now I was having what was on the face of it the time of my life. I was in my mid-twenties, and living for nothing in a nice if scruffy shared house in achingly trendy Camden Town. I was elected in 1980 as full-time NUS Vice-President (Education) and began earning my first real income for doing something I found really exciting and rewarding, developing NUS education policy and campaigns from virtually nothing (the 'movement' hadn't really understood previously that students might have some interest in their education; it was too busy going on about South Africa and the Alternative Economic Strategy), and zapping around the country addressing appreciative audiences of hundreds and sometimes thousands. I was also, when I stopped long enough to notice, falling head over heels for comrade, tentative sexual partner, enthusiastic drug-sharer, and soon fellow NUS executive member Nicky. Over a period of months, the balance of power in our relationship subtly shifted, away from me being the dominant partner in terms of age, and political and sexual status. For the moment, my nominal seniority served to obscure my relative personal weakness and emotional fragility up against this diamond-bright tough cookie. There was a period of a few blessed months when we were more or less equal, into the summer of 1981, revelling in each other's company regardless of who (or, more to the point, what) we were. We'd go swimming in the open air ponds on Hampstead Heath, dry off in the grass and sunshine, then partake of the best ice cream in London at Marine Ices in Chalk Farm. We walked the West Highland Way together, two weeks of rehabilitative exercise and drug-free fresh air and mostly sunshine and glorious Scottish countryside. But there came a point when I began to feel overtaken. My student political career was on the wane, while hers was on the rise. These things mattered among bright, ambitious young people; probably still do.

In the autumn of 1981, Nicky made it clear that our 'aberration' was over. I was aware that she had got close to a number of other NUS women, including out and proud lesbians, but I took our parting hard. Again I felt the indignity of being dumped, but I was also genuinely besotted. I remember a druggy evening, still together but clearly coming apart, at the Hoxton council flat of a mutual friend, actually the CP National Student Organiser at the time (another nice man, but hopelessly out of his depth). Weirdly there was porn on the video-player, courtesy of our host's girlfriend's dodgy brother, but we were too stoned to make a cogent argument against it. Another clear memory of that evening – just as weird because cannabis and cocaine usually had the effect on me of erasing everything afterwards – was listening to the darkest track on the darkest Bruce Springsteen album, predictably titled 'Darkness on the Edge of Town', and thinking how horribly apt, in mood as much as lyrical content. 'Now there's wrinkles around my baby's eyes, and she cries herself to sleep at night', sang the Boss, and I tried to figure out in my own addled mind if the wrinkled crying baby was me or Nicky. Back on my own I listened to lots of other unsuitable music, most unsuitably Joy Division's 'Love will tear us apart'. Another searing memory from that awful time: watching Madness perform at the Rainbow in Finsbury Park at the climax of the Peoples' March for Jobs, taking Nicky back to my flat round the corner halfway through the show, getting down on my knees and sobbing uncontrollably, begging her to come back to me. She gently said no and went back to catch the end of Madness.

At this point I need to introduce another character and another relationship, non-sexual but profoundly and unsettlingly emotional. Also a comrade, but of a very distinct type: born into the party, the child of a noted 'party family' but blessed with talents that would never find any use or outlet in the party's embattled public profile, its plodding organisational routine and always secretive inner life, or its earnest social milieu and limited cultural reach. He's remained a well known public figure, notorious in some circles, a certain David Aaronovitch. He has been described to me by another prominent ex-communist journalist as 'a clever buffoon'. Another mutual acquaintance, who took David into his communal house, reports him answering complaints about not doing his share of domestic chores by saying that his contribution to the household was 'being witty'. More recently my then-MP Charles Clarke told me that David was one of the most cynical people he'd ever met, which from one of the principal architects of New Labour is saying something. David had been an on-off kind of student through the 1970s, expelled from Cambridge for reasons never made clear to me at least (probably just not doing enough work), then doing a history degree at Manchester with lots of time out for a burgeoning career on the NUS Executive. He did six years eventually in NUS, the maximum possible stretch, and was virtually ordered back to Manchester during my sabbatical year by the then NUS President, the communist and later SDP-er Sue Slipman, to finally complete his degree before he could become an NUS 'full-timer'. David was notoriously inactive in the local student union or party branch, and was never caught up in the excitement of CUL or Euro-communism. He seemed to think that being born into the party and bearing a famous party name was enough. We were, like many before and since, charmed but not fooled.

David was elected NUS President at the same time as I was elected Vice-President. We were the two communists in a team of five fulltime elected officials, the last ever elected to the senior NUS posts. At first we worked well together. His declamatory skills and strength of will suited him for his job, and my more analytical and persuasive approach suited me for mine. His ebullience could sometimes get the better of him – as when he declared to a startled NUS Conference, in response to a heckled insult, that he was 'proud to be a wanker' – but I got quite good at spotting and averting the worst of it. We were never really friends – he had a curious social life, quite outside the party, centred on odd (for a communist) pursuits like war-gaming, and he was uneasy around drugs – but we were close political colleagues. I remember a photograph taken at the very end of an NUS Conference, when, virtually alone, David and I had fought off challenges from the ultra left on one side and our increasingly impatient Labour allies on the other, by appealing to the common sense of the body of 'real students' in between. We looked exhausted but happy, leaning into each other on the conference platform. (That would also have been the conference when I earned myself a place on the Provisional IRA's hit-list, by orchestrating resistance to an attempt to get NUS support for the hunger strikes. For the only non-sectarian union in Northern Ireland, with a mass membership of both Protestants and Catholics, it would have been a disaster. I was informed a few days after that I could not safely visit Belfast for six months or so, and that in the meantime Special Branch would be keeping a discreet eye on me.) The other thing about David was that he was an outrageous, not to say compulsive flirt; and his 'lost boy innocence' and oodles of charm brought him lots of wholly willing victims as he cavorted around his NUS fiefdom.

In our second and final year in the NUS leadership I became increasingly unsure of what David was spending his time doing, apart from looking for jobs in the media, and uneasy about some of the decisions he was forcing through the executive. We were plainly losing political control to the bearded Bennite Scotsmen of the National Organisation of Labour Students – which would from this period onwards maintain a stifling stranglehold on the NUS, pretty much up to the present day, in the process turning it into not much more than a rung on the political career ladder. In pursuit of creating a 'legacy', David set about recruiting an all-powerful chief executive to leave behind. That might not have been such a bad idea for an organisation plainly heading for political instability and, quite possibly under Thatcher, irrelevance. The problem was more David's choice of candidate, a failed businessman from the north west of England who turned out to be a disaster, and who lasted in NUS little longer than David and me. The last I heard of him he was Head of Security at Wembley Stadium.

By this time, our final months in office, I had half an eye to my own 'legacy', and decided to challenge aspects of this appointment, which I thought just might be illegal, and were certainly morally questionable. But when I raised these concerns among our comrades and our wider majority group on the NUS executive, David treated the issue as a major test of loyalty, and turned all his charm and guile against me. All but one of the executive – an old friend from Manchester – rallied round David, leaving me totally isolated. Maybe I – ex-Catholic, always inclined to moral black and whites – overstated my case, I don't know. What I do know is that the worst of it for me was that Nicky vociferously sided with David.

Shortly afterwards Nicky stood for election to the post of Vice-President (Education) that I was now relinquishing. She'd have been great, but she lost to a Labour loudmouth. I suspect I was more upset by her defeat than she was.

SYNTHESIS

I left NUS in June 1982, and had a brief and intensely sexual fling with a completely non-political and unquestionably heterosexual woman who picked me up on a train. She was the granddaughter of the psychoanalyst Alfred Adler, whose most famous concept was the inferiority complex. Then I spent six summer weeks in Turin on an EU-funded language course for 'young leaders'. It was just what I needed by way of immediate recuperation, totally away from it all, David and Nicky and the rest of it. I came back to England tanned and rested and conversationally fluent in Italian, and seriously contemplated going back to Italy for good – not least because, unlike in Britain, there still seemed to be some point in the Communist Party. In the meantime I continued to have better sex with a string of women, having realised that I didn't have to fall in love every time, or even feel much for them at all. I was similarly numb when it came to politics. Like David, I had actually done very little in the CP while I was involved in NUS. Comrades in the 'mass movements' were excused pretty much all party activity, except speaking at occasional party meetings and writing the odd article for the party press. We were prototype 'celebrities', I suppose, names for the party to bandy about to show it still counted for something – which, several years into the Thatcherite counter-revolution, it plainly didn't any more, if it ever really had.

I established fitful contact with my local party branch in north London, but made it plain I didn't really want to do anything. I now felt above the grind of leaflet-drops and *Morning Star* sales. At the same time, the party had no obvious use for an emotionally damaged ex-student politician. In the absence of any other available direction I drifted into a career as a 'punk poet' in the burgeoning 'alternative cabaret' circuit, declaiming my own comic verse to upstairs pub rooms and community centres. I did rather well at it, with two or three gigs a week at £30 a time on top of my dole, and more money earned from self-published books. One of these, *The Playbook for Young Adults about Late Capitalism*, sold 3000 copies over Christmas 1983 and topped the *City Limits* Alternative Bestseller list for two weeks in a row. I was filmed for BBC2, performing my deeply cynical 'The Revolution *will* be Televised' outside Channel 4 on Charlotte Street. The same number was included in a hit West End show *Cut and Thrust* produced by Robyn Archer. That was the peak of it. After about eighteen months I got bored, the audiences got drunker and rowdier and less tolerant of anything but stand-up comedy, and the venues and bookshops in which I'd performed and sold my books began to submit to the long dark *Krystallnacht* of Thatcherism. By then my first child was on the way, and I decided I needed a proper grown-up job. But I still had time for my biggest and, for our purposes here, most significant gig of all, a CP jamboree in the summer of 1985 at Alexandra Palace.

The reform drive in the CP had stalled in 1979. After our partial success over the 1977 *BRS* revision, and the zenith of electoral Eurocommunism in Italy, Spain and (to a lesser extent) France, the British Euros made what now looks like the major strategic mistake of turning their reforming zeal onto the party's antiquated internal procedures of 'democratic centralism' and 'recommended lists' and all the other 'administrative measures' of Stalinist discipline. In response, the mainstream of the party was all too ready to turn in on itself, and even more steadfastly ignore the outside world. They voted at the 1979 congress to retain the old structures largely intact, and the most capable Euros went off in a huff. Over the next few years, many either left the party or (like me) found other outlets in student politics and other 'mass movements' or in academia and journalism. *Marxism Today* thrived commercially and politically, even as Marxism and communism were breaking into pieces.

By 1985, the CPGB was visibly dying, but it could still put on a good show. I was asked to organise the 'punk' strand of the 'poetry tent' at Ally Pally, and duly roped in some of my contacts from the cabaret circuit. For some reason, on the day itself we were also asked to perform on the main stage (quite possibly one of the more usual

CP-approved 'stars' hadn't shown up). The punk poetry went really well, booming out over a proper PA system to a hall of 3000 people. The problem came when I approached CP official Nina Temple for payment afterwards. Understandably my collection of punk poets wanted to be paid for two performances, but she would only pay for one (I was expected to forego payment of any kind). The rumour was that the party had blown the ticket money on the briefly chart-topping *a cappella* group The Flying Pickets. I was left to explain to a bunch of outraged (non-communist) punk poets that they were only getting half their money.

I had one more encounter with Nina Temple. I had indeed got a semi-proper job, as a bookseller in Collets London Bookshop on Charing Cross Road. It was a standard transitory position for ex-student party members, and one of the nicest jobs I've ever had, surrounded by bright people and political literature all day. But the company management of Collets, set up by the party in the 1930s but by now (just like the similarly irksome *Morning Star*) firmly under Stalinist control, wanted to close the vibrantly heterodox and commercially viable London Bookshop and concentrate operations on their bigger shop further up the road, where they sold the cheap, heavily subsidised Soviet editions of Marxist classics which kept the whole company afloat. We mounted a really good campaign to save the London Bookshop, including a petition signed by thousands of venerable lefties and an early day motion in Parliament. But when I approached Nina Temple to ask if the party would intervene she would have nothing to do with us, in spite of her credentials as a leading 'Eurocommunist' and anti-Stalinist. The bookshop duly closed, followed not too long after by the whole company (and of course its Soviet sponsors).

By then I'd really had enough of the CPGB. I left in 1985 with a letter to the party's weekly paper *Comment*, citing political objections to the use of Stalinist methods to deal with the Stalinists, but actually I just had better things to do with my life. I distinctly remember the relief of not having to have an opinion about everything – the luxury of indifference. I took on a succession of jobs in the voluntary sector and education before finally arriving in the professional field, the social care of people with HIV/AIDS, where I've made a career over nearly twenty years. But again I'm getting ahead of myself. Time to introduce the third and most probably final love of my life.

I first saw Dina coming down a narrow staircase from the attic offices of the British Youth Council in Somers Town, just north of Euston Road. I was on the BYC executive as a residue of my time in NUS, and she had one of those amorphous 1980s jobs with the word 'development' in the title, meaning your employers didn't really know what they wanted you to do. She was, in the androgynous way of the early 1980s, breathtakingly beautiful, with deep set blue eyes, full eyebrows and high cheekbones. Even better, she had no particular interest in NUS or my recent travails, and knew nothing more about me than that I was vaguely 'important'. When I came back from Italy I wangled a dinner invitation, turned up customarily late, and predictably ended up in her bed. What with my punk poetry and her native north Londoner connections, we were for a little while a pretty cool couple, until domesticity and child-rearing put an end to all that. Thirty years later we're still together, in the curious but delightful 'fine city' of Norwich, having fled London in 1990. Along the way we've had three children, now grown-up and back living in London and establishing careers and homes of their own. It took me a long time to accept that Dina was not particularly political, beyond a vague Labour loyalism and a deep moral sense of fairness and responsibility. This probably has something to do with her own family background, which has its own intrinsic historical interest (and, I have to admit, was part of her appeal for me).

Dina's Dad Fred was born in the south-east German city of Leipzig in 1911 and trained as a printer. His family was heavily political, and he joined the Deutsche Jugend (Young Communist League) in his teens. He ended up a senior DJ functionary in the early 1930s, and had a spell at the Comintern training school in Moscow. He had a way of telling stories which concentrated on incidental details, then suddenly dropped in something quite extraordinary, like the family dinner when he was reciting the menu at a Comintern banquet then happened to mention that he was sitting next to Krupskaya, Lenin's widow. Or the kitten he'd had to keep quiet by shutting in a cupboard in Berlin, then leave behind while he fled over the rooftops. Why? Because the Nazis were breaking down the door to arrest him – which they eventually did. He spent several months in 1935 in Colditz before getting out on a technicality. On a family outing to see Brecht's film *Kuhle Wampe*, he suddenly shouted 'There's my first wife!'. She was a member of the theatre group Rote Megafon, and it was a short-lived party-arranged marriage. Fred got the last plane out of Prague in 1939, hours before the Nazi invasion, arrived in London and in 1940 was promptly interned as an 'enemy alien'. He spent most of the war with other communists in a camp in Canada, then resumed his printing trade back in London (we have a 1950s business card, which says 'German' after his name). He met and married Dina's mum, also German but of a later, post-war expatriate generation, and the rest of his life passed off without much incident. He remained stateless till his very old age, because he was unsure how the GDR – now led by his DJ contemporaries – would receive him. His wife always said that without the party to tell them what to do, Fred and his exiled comrades were adrift and curiously unpolitical. Even after his death in 2007, she continues to tell extraordinary tales about Fred and his family, for example the one about his younger sister Hannah (a Comintern agent in Shanghai) turning down a proposal of marriage from Walter Ulbricht, future GDR leader and 'an odious little man'.

Dina is rightly suspicious of my interest in her family. To a northern English oik like me, it has a certain continental exoticism. But my fascination also says something about the British CP, its insularity bordering on xenophobia, tempered only by its painful awareness that it wasn't really welcome in Britain either. Our CP was a strangely stateless entity, an alien in its own land but with precious little to do with 'comrades from other lands' either, apart from a few intrepid internationalists who had the personal privilege or professional obligation of foreign travel, and the stony-faced apparatchiks who basically became Russian agents. When I came back from summers in Italy in the 1970s and early 1980s and spoke about 'the political situation' at party meetings, I might as well have been talking about the moon. My goodness, a democratic western European country with hundreds of thousands of CP members and millions of communist voters, and some prospect of forming a government! How quaint; now let's get back to the *Morning Star* rota.

Dina and I have got on with our lives together productively and honourably, and for the most part harmoniously and happily. My life before I met her, dwelt upon here at some length, feels for the most part safely 'boxed' and packed away. My personal history has occasionally (as history does) come back to haunt me, usually in the form of a familiar name and face thirty years older (including most recently the Tory leader of Buckinghamshire County Council!). On occasions the past bites. David's successful media career – including stints on *Newsnight*, Radio 4 and most of the 'quality' newspapers – has brought constant reminders of the attention and rewards our society confers on bright, fluent, well-connected but essentially unscrupulous people, as well as the finally painful memories of our time together and (as Dina points out) a measure of envy on my part. Our paths have nearly crossed on several occasions, but I suspect both of us would find an actual reunion excruciating. Nicky went off to the Greenham Common Women's Peace Camp, the great *casus anti-belli* of separatist feminism, and became a full-time lesbian. One Sunday afternoon in 1987 we found ourselves sitting across an aisle in Marine Ices for a painful half hour. Nicky made a literary career of sorts, out of sharply observed but thematically confused lesbian science fiction. This included a spell teaching on the famous MA in Creative Writing at UEA, a course which I myself undertook as a student in 2000. By then I think she'd given up on fiction, or maybe it had given up on her. The last I heard of Nicky was that she was working in 'public affairs', basically running stalls at party conferences and lobbying government on behalf of private companies. Apparently she needed the money. I felt queasy and sad in roughly equal measure. For years I'd have 'Nicky dreams', whose themes alternated between dignified reconciliation and angry severance, but it's been a long time since the last.

'POLICIES AND PERSPECTIVES'

So what am I left with for my ten-year membership of the Communist Party of Great Britain, aside from a bunch of hopefully interesting anecdotes and a vague sense of having been scarred for life? It's a mixed emotional balance sheet, which includes pride in the Italian communists very nearly achieving a truly democratic revolution in the mid-1970s (before the CIA, the Red Brigades and 'rogue elements' in the state murdered both it and Aldo Moro), and in the Russian communists of 'the great patriotic war' as portrayed with truth and sympathy in Vasily Grossman's *Life and Fate*. But there is also shame – at the role of *Marxism Today* and the latter-day 'Eurocommunists' in preparing the ground for New Labour, or at the grey horror of the GDR, of which I got a recent glimpse in the Stasi Museum in Leipzig, quite the creepiest place I've ever been.

Back on the upside, I gained an absolutely fantastic and unparalleled political education in democratic organisation and applied social theory, a 'mass politics' without the corrupting temptations of populist electioneering and parliamentary careerism. This was also for the most part a rigorously secular, honest and analytical politics of action, with very little of the essentially religious proselytising and faith-based 'values' which pass for politics in and around the Labour Party. But all this was offset, particularly after the largely self-inflicted death of the British political left, by very limited prospects for the practical exercise of all those skills and insights. When I look back on my political lifetime, I have a very strong sense of being all dressed up with nowhere to go. During the periods when I have become politically involved since leaving the CP (joining the Labour Party in 1997 and rapidly becoming a city councillor then a council 'cabinet member', then more recently advising the large local Green Party), where I have been most effective and successful has been in my capacity for public speaking, strategic analysis and ability to make constructive proposals, which I got from being a communist. I have also put these skills and others into my work on HIV/AIDS, particularly an understanding of the 'identity politics' which has displaced the traditional class politics of the left (all that time spent with feminists must have done me some good). And my knowledge of historical study and analysis, which comes directly from Marx and (much more so) the great Gramsci, recently saw me through a PhD and a book on *The Politics of New Labour*.

But what about the down sides? I think of all that time spent with essentially disturbed people, some of them outright crazy. You had to be something of a misfit or malcontent to become or remain a communist, but so many of them were simply pathologically at odds with themselves and other people. That's why I've kept in touch with so few ex-comrades – a handful really, who would have probably been friends in any setting – and taken active steps to avoid so many others. God, the bores! The people who can suck all the life out of you in a thirty-second conversation and put nothing back. The almost complete disinclination or inability to listen, among women as well as men. People for whom other people's responses are simply intervals, a breathing space in their own diatribes. Of course I have some of this myself, including a tendency to egotism and pomposity, but at least I recognise it and try to keep it in check. Talking with some of these people when researching for *The Politics of New Labour*, I re-experienced that dull ache and vague sense of contamination that comes from dealing with sticky balls of unresolved neurosis, utter self-absorption within a total lack of awareness of how you come across to other people. People trapped in their own limited obsessions, whose lives had only really taken off when they were in the Communist Party, and had pretty much stood still since it disbanded (and this is not just the 'Stalinists'). So few seem to have thought afresh, taken intellectual risks or really changed their minds about anything for more than twenty years. Stuck in a political rut, a lot of ex-communists have been gripped by a kind of intellectual and emotional paralysis, the party that time forgot. And for all the expansiveness of their 'Marxism' or even 'Gramscism', these were often incredibly narrow, basically uncultured people. When I mention The Blue Nile or the National, Wim Wenders or Flannery O'Connor, Madmen or Richard Yeats, Jeremy Deller or Constructivism – none of them especially obscure cultural references – or even the widely acknowledged and publicised recent golden age in socially aware British theatre, a glazed look comes over their faces until we can get back to talking about the next general election.

So, personally, I don't regret the demise of the CPGB (though I don't really understand it). I do regret most if not all my CP-set emotional entanglements: too much damage to already damaged individuals, myself included. I note with some relief that for all their historical ignorance and lack of political interest, their shallow thinking and attention deficits, young people nowadays have a real talent for friendship and for the most part kindness that far surpasses my generation. They simply don't treat each other with the casual disdain and occasional brutality that we did, even in the minefield of love. One of my son's friends was recently dumped, but told me that this was far easier to live with than doing the dumping; his other friends agreed. In this small detail of emotional transaction, there is substantial historical progress in human affairs. But I also regret that there is no longer a principled, strategically aware and sensibly practical left-wing political organisation for my children and other engaged young people to join and get a political education from, to be formed and matured by, socialised and individuated within, as we were.

Others will, I'm sure, contribute broader assessments of the effects of the CP's absence from recent British history, and of the difference its continued presence might have made. I offer one small, parochial example from my six years involvement in Norwich Labour Party, which I think illustrates the more general impact upon the Labour Party of the loss of its most steadfast and provocative 'critical friend'. It came as a shock when I joined the Labour Party to realise not just that Labourites didn't really like each other, but that they actively *disliked* each other. For example a whole room of people would groan when a particularly garrulous and addled old 'comrade' stood up to speak; while the fact that she was an Asian woman among mostly white men seemed (to me at any rate) to add more than a whiff of racism and sexism to the basic rudeness of it. The formal business of Labour Party meetings was perfunctory and overwhelmingly administrative; the actual political business took the form of small plotting huddles in the bar outside, where deals would be done on votes and elections whose results made no sense in terms of what was said and done out in the open. Real physical violence was not by any means unheard of, and often threatened. The internal atmosphere of the Communist Party might have sometimes got heated and polarised, especially towards the end, but at least in my experience it was always respectful and essentially *principled*. And for all the strictures of democratic centralism, national CP officials usually treated local branches with a kind of inverse deference, not least because they understood that they were the party's main point of contact with the real world of 'ordinary people'.

The most serious effect of the CP's demise on the 'inner life' of the Labour Party derives from the lack of political competition and Labour's effective monopoly over sensible left-wing politics. While the CP existed, there was always a reasonable left-wing alternative to the Labour Party, as I found in south Leeds and Manchester in the 1970s. Prior to that, as is shown for example in Hugh Gaitskell's relationship with his constituency party in Leeds, Labour's leaders had to work really hard to keep their 'small band' of party workers and supporters on board, with a steady diet of encouragement, cajoling, flattery and outright patronage. That didn't come easy to Gaitskell, the archetypal Hampstead intellectual and cosmopolitan *bon viveur*, but he understood the 'sacrifice' required by parliamentary and government office, including frequently putting south Leeds people up in his own house on their jaunts to London. The local CP branch (which I later joined) was large and lively, and regularly made unwelcome suggestions of 'joint action' or less subtle appeals to disgruntled Labourites.

Now, without the CP locally or nationally, there is nothing to make Labour's leaders cultivate, appease or even respect their own party membership, which not surprisingly has halved since 1997. The balance of power in the organisation's 'moral economy', as well as its more formal decision-making procedures, has radically shifted towards the centre. In my time in Norwich Labour Party, 'visitations' by national figures were few and far between – a couple of young men in suits explaining the benefits of telephone canvassing to these hardened door-knockers, the Treasury minister Steven Timms trying to keep his huge legs to himself in a tiny committee room, Lord Derry Irvine smiling down at us with a look of utter contempt when someone dared to mention his office wallpaper, Charles Clarke blustering through every challenge, even when he was the only person in a GC meeting of 150 who supported the war in Iraq. And such leaders' written memoirs make plain their disgust at the 'complete lunatics' out there in the country beyond Westminster. This deep disdain for Labour people (as well as for 'old' Labour politics) has been a major and barely noted element in the temperamental mix of New Labour. Is it any wonder that most sensible people, especially the young, have responded in kind and deserted organised left-wing politics? And that the only people left at Labour's 'grass roots' are indeed the mad and the sad, oblivious to their leaders' contempt and with nothing better to do...

Otherwise, all there seems to be in twenty-first century Britain is a conceptually amorphous but socially exclusive, perpetually agonised 'cultural left' clustered around the universities and the readership of the *Guardian*, and a small but busy band of unreconstructed Trots and anarchists staging historical re-enactments of supposed glory days. It makes great television but lousy politics, and deepens the isolation of the political left and the continuing hegemony of Thatcherism. An immensely valuable historical chain of constructive resistance – which linked the Paris Communards and Marxist *diaspora*, the free thinkers and free lovers of Victorian England, the pre-Stalinist Bolsheviks, the great anti-fascist alliances of the 1930s and 1940s and the accompanying 'Popular Front of the mind', the post-war 'democratic communism' in Italy and even parts of Eastern Europe, the CP dissidents who formed the first New Left and CND, the CP-steered national liberation movements of the former colonies, the best of '1968' and the 'new social movements' of personal liberation, and the promising but doomed flowering of Euro-communism – has been broken, apparently forever. The Communist Party of Great Britain was a grand and not particularly glorious historical failure, but the best of it was the best of British politics. It is deeply missed, and remains to be properly mourned.

I struggle for a conclusion to my personal story – hopefully there's plenty more to come. What comes through now are a number of lessons, or perhaps homilies. The first concerns the difficulty, perhaps impossibility, of real friendship in politics or any other sphere of public life. It is so hard to conduct truly caring and sometimes loving relationships under any kind of public scrutiny. The spotlight is just too harsh and unforgiving, the competition too fierce and divisive. Most occupations bring with them some kind of professional code, including clear boundaries between the public and the private, but for my generation of left-wing political activists there was no such readymade code, not least because we decried the 'careerism' of professional politics and the categories of patriarchy. We made profound discoveries along the way, but also profound mistakes. And we were so very young. I left my family home at 18 and rarely returned; in my head I'd left at 13. We saw and did so much, through that historically momentous period spanning the 1960s, 1970s and 1980s, that it's no surprise our young lives felt so bewilderingly entangled.

I and many of the people I knew have spent much of the rest of our lives trying to disentangle it all (including, in his own very public way, David Aaronovitch). It's too late to undo the damage, which we will live with for the rest of our lives, but there is also a kind of wisdom to be found from identifying its causes and symptoms; a maturity of understanding. Also, as you get older you see the continuities as well as disruptions, especially with your childhood, which as a young adult you tend to disregard, desperate to grow up and leave it all behind. And in that process of mature recollection and reflection, there is a chance to reintegrate your life as a whole experience, and to tell your own story with historical truth and social meaning. I am well aware of my own tendency to solitariness; I have never really understood or trusted other people, and that has a lot to do with the early death of my father and several 'significant others' during my childhood. I suspect that all of us who have 'loved and lost', i.e. pretty much everybody, have some sympathy for Sartre's notion that 'hell is other people'. And that's the final irony of my personal commitment to communism: that it represented my own protracted struggle to overcome my profound dislike of others.

We will rebuild our country ten times more beautiful

Lorna Reith

What to do on a cold January New Year's bank holiday Monday? My partner Quentin Given and I decide on the Museum of London. We have not been for years and the place has undergone lots of changes and has some new displays. We skip most of the Stone Age, the Romans and the Plague and spend a bit longer with the Victorians, the Suffragettes and the Second World War. But it's the sixties, seventies and eighties that draw us in. Having reminisced about Biba and the Kinks we move along the displays to the Queen's Silver Jubilee. There's an SWP 'Stuff the Jubilee' sticker and then a panel about the People's Jubilee at Alexandra Palace – also attributed to the SWP.

It's at this point that I realise that the Communist Party still matters to me. The CP organised the People's Jubilee and I'm proud of that. I don't want some other organisation getting the credit. I do also have a concern about the re-writing of history – I suspect this is part of the party's legacy as well. As soon as we get home e-mails are dispatched to the museum. An apology is received and a correction is promised. So if you're visiting the Museum of London (and I can recommend it) please check this has been done.

It's not that I think about the party very often. But despite being in the Labour Party for over fifteen years, whenever I use the term 'the party' I always mean the CP. I don't know if this is just because it came first or because it was my political home and reference point during my formative years, or both.

NOW

I've been Deputy Leader of the London Borough of Haringey for some years and I took on the responsibility of Cabinet Member for Children in the wake of the Baby Peter tragedy. Life's been busy. Much of it in the glare of the tabloids, where simple things like a DVD on children's centres for traveller families will result in headlines prefaced with *'Baby P council wastes money on...'* Getting to grips with child protection services was a steep learning curve for me, and I've not had much time to step back and think about the wider political and ideological landscape. It is also my experience that the Labour Party generally doesn't do this very much; this is where I miss the party.

Currently, like many councils, we are involved in making ferocious cuts in services, closing residential care homes, day centres and children's centres, reducing our youth service by 75 per cent and generally seeing much of the good services we've built up over the Labour government years being dismantled. We had to take £41m (about 17 per cent) out of the budget last year – with direct job losses in the Council of between 700 and 1000 posts – and there are still substantial savings to be made over this year and next – £84m in total.

So, should I be doing this or should I be outside protesting? Labour's cuts are my cuts. Are they any better than cuts made by a council officer or by the opposition? Am I managing people's expectations rather than raising them? Did I imagine this is how I would end up?

I have lived in Haringey since leaving university, and at my present address, on a council estate in the ward I represent in Tottenham, for over thirty years. For me, living in the area I represent is important and is a way of being in touch with the reality of working-class people's lives. Tottenham is a severely deprived constituency, home to an extraordinary diverse range of people from all over the globe. There are some 197 languages spoken in the borough, and a high population turn-over, as people move through. A quarter of the households in England living in temporary accommodation are in the upper Lea Valley, of which Tottenham is part. And now that the Coalition government have decided that people on benefits shouldn't be allowed to live in Central London we're expecting an additional influx of poorer families.

THEN

I joined the Communist Party as a student in the early 1970s from a politically left family background. I was attracted by the revolutionary and slightly romantic appeal of the CP, and although my parents were Labour Party members they took the *Daily Worker* and I'd grown up within a communist/socialist political tradition. Our house was always the Labour Party committee rooms at election time, and there was a polling station at the end of the road. I knew all the local streets – not like other kids because I played in them, but because I delivered leaflets. From an early age my hand-writing skills were honed addressing envelopes. I had a good grounding in the class nature of voting patterns, how to run an election machine and fund-raising activities like jumble sales and bazaars. Through the Socialist Sunday School (no religion) we raised money for Medical Aid for Vietnam through plays, in one of which I played the part of a tree in a Vietnamese legend. At no point in my childhood had I knowingly eaten South African produce.

My student political involvement matched the issues of the time. Early mornings handing out milk to school children in Lancaster – to protest the move that earned her the moniker 'Thatcher milksnatcher'. I discovered feminism, supported the gay liberation front and demands for greater student involvement in our learning.

Its funny how what seems a small choice, made almost accidentally, can affect your whole life. Our CP branch on campus gave me the choice of becoming *Morning Star* organiser or Chile Solidarity Campaign representative. I chose the latter and remained closely involved, working with refugees and visiting Chile, until we closed the Campaign down in the early 1990s.

My student experience wasn't uncommon; universities were opening up to young people from a wider range of backgrounds, many the first in their family to go on to higher education. And post-1968, student unrest across Europe and in the USA meant heady days for students at home. Many weekends were spent on a coach to

London for a demonstration – Lancaster was a long way away. One very clear lesson from the CP stays with me. As a student body we'd gone into occupation, taking over the Senate building. The trigger had been the refusal of a hardship payment to a student in debt, but as always there were a range of underlying issues and a keenness by political activists for some direct action. We were all caught up in the excitement of the event when a senior party member was despatched from the North West district to give us the line. We sat in a room and he grilled us about our exit strategy – which of course we didn't have. We were brought down to earth and began planning the steps which would end the occupation, win some concessions and ensure that no students were sent down.

All in all it was a bit unreal, though like many of my generation, I thrilled to the recent anti-tuition fees student demonstrations. I still feel guiltily privileged not to have had to pay for my university education.

Having left university I returned to London and started work for a housing charity while continuing my involvement in the Chile Solidarity Campaign and then a wide range of campaigns. At work I took on the obligatory role of shop steward, then chair of the union branch and, having moved into the flat where I still live, became active in the London tenants' movement. With CSC always there in the background, my life included CND, visits to Greenham Common and leading a major anti-road building campaign. Throughout this the CP was my political home. Everything I did was informed by being in the party. In wider movements I sought out fellow CP members, both within the UK and internationally. Though there were lots of apparently single-issue campaigns, as party members we were informed and brought together by an over-arching political understanding and ideology.

I was, however, perpetually frustrated at the hierarchy within the party, where trade union activity reigned supreme (and certain unions within that). Maybe we could have done more in these other movements if there'd been resources put in. Or maybe it's just that we did achieve quite a lot but it was never properly acknowledged. One thing I am able to say now is that we definitely missed opportunities to influence what happened at a local government level. Of course this wasn't the case everywhere, and some CP branches

(Hackney and Lambeth spring to mind) did intervene successfully at a local level. More generally, however, because the CP hadn't been in power in local councils, we lacked awareness of how local government worked and how best to influence decisions. The over-concentration on trade union work probably didn't help either. This lack of knowledge about how power works and how to influence decisions was equally true at a national level. I certainly had more influence over legislation which affected thousands of people when I became a chief executive of a national disability charity than I had ever done in the Communist Party.

So what was it about being in the party? How were we different from other political parties and groups? What did I learn? Well I'd go back to *The British Road to Socialism*. Although some in the party became almost dismissive of it, maybe because the language it used wasn't that of academic political discourse, it did set out the way in which party members worked in society at large. It was about widening and deepening democracy, and understood the importance of building collective values and solidarity (or cohesion if you want a more modern word) within society.

For me the basic premises were about working to create broad-based movements, building alliances, starting from where people are and not where you'd like them to be. Understanding the need to consolidate even quite small gains and embed them. Take people with you and have them be part of the success. Recognising that leadership is vital but it doesn't have to be overt and is not about using the campaign as a recruitment tool – ordinary people will see through this, feel used and resent you. Overall I feel the CP was less instrumental in its approach than the ultra-left or indeed the Labour Party.

One thing that remains unresolved for me was how much this way of working was really the ideology of the party and how much just a consequence of not being in power. Examples from Eastern Europe would, unfortunately, seem to suggest the latter. Nevertheless, it was a style of politics that informed all my community-based work and was so much a part of me that I automatically took it into the Labour Party.

This period was also one in which debates on feminism, anti-racism and identity politics were all around. Though obviously not confined to the party, they provided an opportunity for the party to do something it did well – encourage ideological discussion beyond its own ranks. Intellectual discussion about political theories is not really part of ward level Labour Party culture, though no doubt it does go on in some areas. There is a gap that the Party used to fill. In fact I sometimes feel I stopped thinking twenty years ago, and now just absorb and process information. The party enabled an understanding of class politics and identity politics, as well as structure and strategy. And for us strategy was about changing society not winning elections.

WHAT

Being part of an international movement was always part and parcel of being in the CP. Branch discussions would almost always include updates and views on what was happening elsewhere in the world. Whenever you met another comrade you could be confident they would know about the major international issues of the time – Vietnam, Chile, South Africa, Nicaragua, Grenada, national liberation struggles across the globe. Different political streams within the party described themselves in international terms. I attended party schools in the former Yugoslavia and in Italy and like many others sought out communist events and contacts when on holiday – from the *Fete de l'Humanité* in France to a festival in Heraklion, Crete. Party events in the UK were often international in character, with invited speakers from sister parties abroad.

I was always conscious of an ambivalence about the role of the USSR. I knew that people in the ANC, in Chile, in Vietnam and in national liberation movements across the world partly depended on support from the USSR and eastern block countries. These countries were also a place of refuge – providing university education and medical treatment for many thousands of political activists as well as a home to those who had to leave their own country. Yet I was also openly critical of the repression in Eastern Europe and supportive of movements like Charter 77 in Czechoslovakia.

As representatives of the Chile Solidarity Campaign, I and my partner visited Chile in 1986 – arriving just after an attempt on

Pinochet's life, and finding ourselves in the middle of the resulting clampdown and curfew. Chilean Communist Party members looked after us, set up meetings with unions and human rights organisations, arranged prison visits and took us to shanty towns and indigenous people's groups. The risks were high, particularly for them. On several occasions our various meetings ran beyond the curfew time but still they got us home safely. In such circumstances – absence of electoral avenues and widespread human rights abuses – the Chilean CP, like our comrades in South Africa, had set up an armed wing. It was they who had been responsible for the failed assassination attempt on Pinochet, and there was evidence of their work (blown up electricity pylons being the most common example) all around. But, where it was possible to conduct more ordinary political struggle they did so in much the same way that we did in the UK. Building broad coalition movements, involving trade unions (which were largely political party rather than industry based), human rights organisations, residents associations, shanty town associations, students and all opposition parties. While there we visited the Christian Democrat student leader in prison in Valparaiso, a young women from the ultra-left party in the women's prison in Coronel (near Concepcion), and in the south, in Valdivia, a Socialist Party student who had been just been released from prison, having been badly tortured.

It is this international element that for me is missing in the local and regional Labour Party. In my own constituency, Tottenham, we have many Labour Party members who have come from other countries, so there is an element of international politics, but it's very much limited to the issues arising from the country or region they are from, rather than a way of understanding the world and our place in it. Obviously there are Labour Party members who are internationalist in that way, but it's not part of the life blood of the organisation the way it was with the CP.

In the bottom of my wardrobe I have a plastic bag containing a chunk of Berlin wall along with some wire from the fence at Greenham Common. Years pass and I forget they are there and then come across them again and have to remind myself what they are. On my kitchen wall is a poster of Vietnamese women in a rice field. It's been there for over thirty years, faded and pasted to the wall. Across the top is a quote from Ho Chi Min 'We will rebuild our country ten times more beautiful'. It still inspires me. More so now as we try and rebuild post-riots Tottenham, which, unlike Vietnam, never started out beautiful.

I was a member of the London District Committee for some years and also convened various internal party groups, examples being 'New Thinking on Welfare' and the Party housing group. I was a CP candidate for election to the European Parliament in 1989. It was great fun as well as being hard work, and all the hustings meetings and leafleting may well have helped increase the left vote (Labour took the seat and the Greens did well), but looking back I'm not at all sure why we stood. Especially as events developed in Tiananmen Square and formed an unforgettable and tragic backdrop to the election.

I was never on the Party Executive Committee, a fact which landed me with chairing the appeal panels for those members who were expelled by the Executive. Not a role I felt comfortable in, since I wanted the party to be less rigid and more open to internal debate. But for me it was a question of applying the existing rules, and in particular making them apply to a group of people who didn't want the party to change and become more open. Through the party I got toughened up politically and personally and learned how to organise. Transferable skills I took into the Labour Party.

DEMOCRATIC LEFT

I was very clearly in what was called the Eurocommunist wing of the party and at one point hoped the party would make the breakthrough into a popular and broad based organisation with an electoral future. Like many others, I looked to the Italian Party as an example.

But in the end I supported the party's dissolution. I felt it was tarnished as a brand and that we carried too much baggage. We were too associated with parties and states in Eastern Europe, and more latterly China, and our activities were inevitably prefaced with an explanation that despite having the same name as them we were different. Our age demographic was against us – we had many wonderful older comrades and then the post-68 generation, but little in between and none bringing up the rear. Recruitment had no doubt always been difficult, but, beset by internal disputes, and in the midst of a more general move away from political party membership, we were rapidly growing smaller and less influential.

At the time I found it inconceivable that there should be no replacement organisation for the CP. Now, with the benefit of hindsight, I think maybe we should have called it a day. However, I became a founding member of Democratic Left and convinced myself that DL would be a genuine replacement with a newer style of democratic politics. But as we all now know it didn't survive.

Insufficient numbers for a start, and although this sounds like stating the blindingly obvious, it is nevertheless true that DL didn't even capture all (eligible) former party members. Discounting those who set up the CPB, there were others who chose this moment to join the Labour Party or the Greens or Plaid Cymru. Others concentrated their efforts in trade union work or campaigning organisations, including the emerging environmental movements. Then there were those who had reached a point in their lives where they no longer had the energy to take part. Here the age profile is relevant. Some of the older comrades no doubt felt that enough was enough; they were not about to throw themselves into an uncertain new venture. Some of the post-68 generation were into starting families and careers and had little spare capacity. So DL started small, and although it did attract some non-party people I think it was hindered by a lack of clarity about its mission and role. DL could so easily be all things to all people, and despite trying not to be defined as against the old CP this was partly inevitable. There were no longer any clear international political links, and, deliberately, it lacked the discipline of a party.

Should the dissolution have taken place earlier? Would this have made a difference? Personally I think not. In fact, I tend to think Democratic Left was in advance of its time. Maybe if it had come into being five years ago instead of twenty it would have taken naturally to organising via Facebook and Twitter, and would have taken off as a movement.

THE LABOUR PARTY

For me there was a need for something over-arching, something that looked at society as a whole and sought change (albeit in a modest and reforming sort of way) and which, like the CP, looked to protect and improve the lot of ordinary people. The Labour Party is not a substitute for the wide range of what we called single issue campaigns, and I continued to be involved in many of these, but for me the Labour Party has provided a framework that linked these other concerns. Although at the beginning my Labour Party membership was pretty token, it still felt good to belong to a political party. I welcomed the fact it was a broad church and never felt the need to automatically defend the party leadership or particular policies.

During the latter years of the last Tory government I was Chief Executive of a national disability charity. I was able to use my political judgement and experience and contribute to the building of coalitions of voluntary organisations, the TUC and direct action groups. Combining this with work across all the political parties within parliament, the disability movement successfully (after thirteen attempts) saw the Disability Discrimination Act come onto the statute book. Together we also fought off many moves to cut back on disability benefits – including ones initiated by the incoming Blair government. For me this type of campaign work came naturally – a CP legacy.

Becoming a local councillor happened almost by accident. A by-election came up in the ward in which I live and a Labour councillor asked me to stand. It was Christmas so I said I'd think about it. I'd not put my name forward before so I wasn't on the 'panel' of potential candidates, and I wasn't that sure it was something I wanted to do. Unknown to me there was some disquiet on the part of people whose names were on the panel, some of whom had stood unsuccessfully in the previous election, and my fellow councillor had to argue the case for my name to go forward. After this I couldn't really let him down so I went for the seat, was selected by the local party, won the by-election and have been re-elected by the people of Tottenham Hale ever since. Haringey is a Labour administration where the opposition are Liberal Democrats. There are two parliamentary seats, one Labour (Tottenham) and one Liberal Democrat (Hornsey and Wood Green).

I spent some months as a back-bencher learning the ropes then became chair of a Scrutiny Committee for a year. I then moved into the Cabinet and later became Deputy Leader. In addition I have held various portfolios, and am currently the Lead for Children. I try to apply what I learned in CP to my everyday politics – at a ward level dealing with constituents, and at Cabinet leadership level.

So what's the internal life of the Labour Party like? I can really only give a perspective as a councillor in power, where we run the administration. It is time consuming and quite narrowly focused and generally more about managing expectations than changing the world. When Labour was in government we had some access to ministers, including our local MP, David Lammy. But, with some exceptions, the Blair administration was dismissive of local government. On many occasions we were completely ignored – even when the number of Labour councils in London was painfully low. I can remember an occasion when Gordon Brown, as prime minister, visited a sports project on the council estate where I live. The event was organised by Spurs, who run the project. I attended with the leader of the Council. Gordon was polite, though clearly not at ease in such situations, but his minders were rude, dismissive and arrogant, and made me ashamed to be associated with the party.

At local branch level life is pretty dull. Certainly there isn't the level of debate there used to be in the CP. One problem, which might have bedevilled the CP as well had it continued, is that the structure hasn't modernised, so there are lots of meetings with no obvious purpose. Not surprisingly the vast majority of members don't attend meetings, and indeed it's hard to think why they should. I get regular information from the LP via email and I imagine this suits most members. In my area, ward meetings tend to be a mix of councillors, who are obliged to attend, and older and low-income members who don't have internet access. The bottom line is that the LP has always primarily been there to win elections – which is what engages most members – and then, if successful, to run an administration.

There are now signs of the LP doing some more serious thinking about the involvement of ordinary members. This is part of coming to terms with the general election defeat and resilience of the Coalition government, but also signifies Ed Miliband's different approach.

I have retained my respect for and understanding of the role of community activists, and people who are political but not members of a political party. Not only am I happy for campaigns to be led by people or groups other than the LP but believe this is often better. Though I have to say this isn't a perspective always shared by my LP colleagues.

It was interesting to see how my LP colleagues split when it came to the referendum on the voting system. To me it had to be a 'Yes' vote – even if the Alternative Vote option on offer wasn't ideal. AV would be a step in the direction of a more democratic system and would allow a better reflection of the electorate's views. But amongst my fellow LP members were many for whom democracy didn't matter – what mattered was winning elections.

Many of the friendships I made through the party have been sustained since and provide a source of political grounding for me. These are people whose opinions I trust, and whose views and perspectives are always of interest. I spot the names of former comrades in the press all the time – and not just in the obituary columns. It's interesting how many of them provide constant reference points in current political debates.

I'm not tribal in my membership of LP, but I'm not going anywhere else either. I have no great desire to be an MP – I have a role I'm happy with. Interestingly that's something where there is a clear difference to the CP – it was generally free of career politicians. I can spot them now, though less than when Labour was in government. Bright young things with no obvious ideology at all and certainly no link or understanding of the labour movement. People you can imagine being in almost any party.

Why is there so little evidence of the CP in modern political life? Is it because those of us who were members now feel embarrassed and never mention it? I confess that I have moments when I'm one of those. But other times I'm quite proud of my past. Has the culture disappeared because we're dissipated as a group of former members – gone into too many different places? I suppose there weren't that many of us anyway and the age profile would be against us.

At the level of central and local government services we face a full-scale dismantling of the public sector, the impact of massive public expenditure cuts and the class nature of that impact. There is a desperate need for local broad-based campaigns. In areas like mine, where Labour runs the local council, such campaigns have to clearly target central rather than local government. In practice, the local

Labour Party isn't sufficiently organised (outside of the council) and ends up ceding ground to the ultra- left or to individual organisations concentrating on specific aspects of the cuts. At a local level there isn't any longer a trade union movement beyond the public sector and I suspect this is true elsewhere.

This is also territory where a CP would have had an influence. The trade union movement is now almost solely a public sector phenomenon, and is often treated with embarrassment by the Labour Party leadership. Where is the Labour Party voice that says that being a trade union member is a good thing? How often do you hear senior Labour figures publicly trying to recruit people to join a union or suggesting that the private sector needs to be unionised?

The CP would have provided that crucial link with left politics, bridging the gap between pursuit of sectional interest – which is what trade unions are designed to do – and the wider interests of ordinary working-class people. But there is a much bigger political gap which the CP might have filled, and where it is much missed. Where now are the agencies seeking a transformation of society? Not just better services, greater efficiency and a more equal distribution of resources, but a fundamental change in both the values by which society is organised and the allocation of power in that society. Where is the political articulation of the need for a fundamental change in the relationship between the developed and developing world?

The situation is still as it was

Stuart Hill

There is, I suppose, a kind of continuity to this story. It sometimes feels as though I have been fighting the same battles, and against the same people, for over forty years – inside the Party, in UNISON, with local authority bureaucracy and inside the Labour Party – against establishments that are privileged, bureaucratic, undemocratic and barely accountable.

I have always drawn a lot of my ideas about democracy from communists I have known, selfless individuals who didn't do it for money or position but because they knew what was right. This wasn't simply an instinctive thing; they understood the forces that they were opposing, that time and time again the odds were stacked against them. I remember an Iranian comrade who went back to Iran after the fall of the Shah. He said that he thought his country stood a chance under Khomeini; on the other hand he knew that there was a good chance that he would end up being tortured and killed. But he was going back as a known communist to try to do his bit. I never heard from him again.

If I was asked to describe my politics now, I would call myself a revolutionary democrat. This seems to me now more important than terms like socialist or communist. The person I most identify with is Thomas Paine, a revolutionary in more than one revolution. He was always prepared to cross the establishment in order to further and deepen democracy.

YCL

I was born in Middlesbrough in 1950. My father was a foundry-worker and a T&G shop steward. He was a pretty tough-man's sort of bloke, nicknamed Fag-Ash because he always had a gravity-defying Woodbine hanging from his lip. My mother was a professional dancer and singer from the age of fourteen until she stated having kids – six of us. It was a typical working-class family, except that we were brought up in a boarding house for working men. My mother ran the place. Both my parents were traditional Labour voters, intelligent observers but not remotely interested in being active. They both joined the Labour Party when they were much older, but they would never go to any meetings.

When I was fourteen I wanted to be a scientist, inspired by Harold Wilson's vision of a technological revolution. But I was soon more interested in history and politics. The crucial issue for me was the war in Vietnam. This politicised me. I had a huge admiration for the Vietnamese people. The first organised activity I was ever involved in was Teesside Medical Aid for Vietnam. Me and my best mate from school were the chair and secretary (and only members). We started collecting for people in Vietnam and raised quite a lot of money. I was arrested for collecting at Darlington Dog Show because we didn't have a collector's licence. My collection tins were confiscated by the police. Eventually, they must have felt sorry for me, and gave me back the money I had collected. Another time I was 'taken into custody' was on the steps of King Street; after being threatened with a truncheon by a thuggish PC in the interview room we were released without charge. The last time I was arrested over Vietnam was at the time of the Christmas bombing of Hanoi. Sharing a police van with a huge Alsatian that seemed to want to eat me was scary. I was convicted for obstruction, for handing out leaflets in front of a flower-bed on Linthorpe Road. An anonymous well-wisher paid my fine. I remember Bruce Sanderson, arrested at the same time, having his head smashed repeatedly against the charge room wall by a sadistic copper. It was awful to have to watch, helpless to intervene. Bruce later became a national union official in TASS. The police had refused to arrest a Stockton comrade, despite him demanding to be arrested. He was a well-known Second World War veteran who had had his legs blown off fighting Fascism. Even in those days the police were image-conscious.

When I was fifteen I decided to investigate the local political scene by attending meetings of the various political parties. The Conservatives had a speaker who talked about life insurance to teenagers. The Young Liberals did not seem to meet. When I asked about the Labour Party Young Socialists, the full-time Labour agent, Councillor Charles Shopland, gave me the third degree. In the end he told me to come back in twelve months. Meanwhile, he said I could help deliver election leaflets if I wanted. When I turned up to help, he told me, and all the volunteers, that the purpose of knocking on doors was *not* to persuade people to vote Labour, it was to identify Labour supporters who could later be mobilised to vote. It was as though the world was ideologically fixed and that voters never change their minds. I thought even then that it was stupid not to try to engage with people. How can you persuade people to change their mind or even to motivate them to come out and vote if you are not going to talk politics with them? That was my first experience of the Labour Party, forty-five years ago.

Lastly, I went along to a meeting of the Young Communist League. The speaker was George Short, a graduate of the Lenin School. It was pretty boring marxist economics, but it was at least about politics. I suppose I might never have gone again but for my admiration of the Vietnamese people. The Vietnamese people were led by Communists, and, while I didn't expect the CPGB to be quite so heroic, they belonged to the same international movement. Remember, the Party was resolute in its support of the Vietnamese people. Whenever I travelled down to Vietnam Solidarity Campaign demonstrations in London, I would come across YCL members. On the other hand, the various Trotskyite parties were always so critical of the Vietnamese. So, despite all its evident weaknesses, I joined the YCL when I was fifteen. The day after my eighteenth birthday, I joined the Party.

We were a mixed bunch of people, mostly working-class. We were actively involved in rent strikes and selling the *Morning Star*. Ernie Jones stood for Parliament and Jim Smith for the council. Both worked for ICI. This was the period leading up to the Prague Spring.

At the time I was fairly ambivalent about the Prague Spring because, although there were some attractive things about what the Czechs were trying to do, I was uncertain with all the Brown Book propaganda about counter revolutionaries and the role of the CIA. However, I quickly came round to the view that it was important that Communist Parties should develop in their own way. I think now that the Prague Spring was the last real chance we had of reforming the socialist countries. It was a tragedy that it was crushed.

The YCL on Teesside was a thriving organisation when I joined. But, within a matter of a few months, almost everybody had left. It was just one of those things with young people. Some were off to university, like Martin Levy to Cambridge, some left to look for work, and in next to no time there was virtually no-one left in the YCL, just me and my best two mates from school, Dave Wedlake and 'Hedge', alias Andrew Harland.

Though the Party was small and not very important in Britain, it was still part of an international movement. I drew a feeling of strength and moral support from that. In different parts of the world the communist movement was making real progress and was helping the national liberation movements in the Third World. The Soviet Union might not have been a bastion of socialist democracy, but it was the intellectual (and often military) arsenal of many liberation movements around the world. The Soviets played a crucial role in Vietnam.

NUPE

I was interviewed by the LSE to study Economics, but got three pretty crummy A-levels grades. Then my father was made redundant. My parents had split up and I felt I had to earn some money to help out. I kept on my summer job working as a road-sweeper for Middlesbrough Council. Later I was promoted to a bin-man. When they needed someone who could write and count, they asked me to work in the office as the depot clerk. That summer job just kept on going. It was about ten years before the lads stopped calling me 'the student'.

In less than three months I was elected a NUPE shop steward. At the time most of the bin-men were in the GMB or the T&G. I helped fill out the forms for the new starters, so NUPE's membership rose consistently. Soon one of the senior managers came down to the depot to tell me I could choose a career in local government or I could be active in the union, but not both. My boats were burnt before I even started with the council.

When I was in my early twenties I was elected to the Trades Council Joint Consultative Committee, a big mouthful but actually a sub-committee of the TUC General Council. This also gave me a seat on the regional TUC executive. My election caused tremendous friction with my employer. I needed to be off work for all sorts of meetings. In the 1970s there was a determined attempt to sack me. Whether it was anti-communism or because I was active in the union, I don't know, but two things happened in response. First, the bin-men threatened all-out strike action. Second, the certainty of a major stoppage contributed to a split in the Labour group, and a body of progressive councillors under Mike Carr replaced the old leadership of Walter Ferrier. The Law of Unintended Consequences!

I had been elected Secretary of the Middlesbrough Trades Council in 1972. The full council met twice a month, and in between the executive committee met. I had to send out minutes and notices of every meeting to everyone! I used to spend hours and hours in the early hours writing envelope after envelope because we didn't have word processors or even sticky labels – I had a typewriter but it was quicker by hand.

When I joined the union, in 1969, at least 80 per cent of the membership was women but there were no women on the National Executive and no women full-time officials. It was a dreadful situation but it was challenged within NUPE by leaders like Bernard Dix and Alan Fisher. I was heavily involved in the battle to get rid of the old retired caretakers who had dominated the union. The national leadership introduced the idea of five seats on the executive reserved for women. After this battle was won I became involved in the much more difficult battle to persuade the five women who were on these reserved seats to stand for the 'general' seats. What had been a breakthrough had quickly become a blockage. The five elected women pulled up the drawbridge because they didn't want to help the forces of change by getting more women on the executive. It was a really important battle and it was bitterly fought over. It led, eventually, to the majority of Unison's National Executive being women by the rules adopted. I was proud to be one of the nine people whose signatures brought Unison into existence. In 1992, I was elected the last National Vice President of NUPE, just before the merger that created Unison.

NUPE had a proud record, particularly within the Northern Region. We had a women's network that was pretty dynamic and did all sorts of original things. But the wider trade union movement, especially in the North East, was pretty dreadful in lots of ways. It has not changed very much. The shipyards and mines have gone, but their macho culture endures.

THE PARTY

Most members were either 'Party' or 'Trade Union Comrades'. I was always both. The union took up most of my time but I was also trying to build the Party on Teesside and in the Northern District. I was also involved in the Party's international work – I went to the World Federation of Democratic Youth Festival in Berlin representing Middlesbrough Trades Council, or its Youth Section).

I was elected to the Party's executive committee in my early twenties. I think I was put on partly because I was from the North East and partly because of my involvement in NUPE and on the trades councils movement. As a newly elected member I was able to visit Mongolia, an amazing country, and share experiences with Russian, Cypriot and Portuguese comrades.

Internationalism was in the DNA of almost all Party members regardless of whatever differences they might otherwise have. I was in Derry the year after the massacre, 1973, with a British labour movement delegation. There was a Liverpool docker, Corby steelworker, Sheffield engineer, Scottish miner and me, the clerk from Middlesbrough Council's Cleansing Depot at Lloyd Street. I think we were all Party members but representing our respective union organisations or Trades Councils. The Provos provided security for the group whilst we were in Derry. It was heavy at times. I remember running out the back door of a pub when someone shouted 'Car

Bomb!' When separated in the confusion of the day from my comrades I was 'jumped' by three British soldiers. One rammed a pistol in my spine as they spread my legs and banged my head against a wall. When they heard my English accent they became polite and friendly. It was quite surreal. I was impressed by the courage, optimism and humour of the Civil Rights people. It took real guts to be on the streets knowing what the British Army was capable of.

Later in the same year I was at the World Youth Festival in Berlin. There was a fair contingent from Middlesbrough – Jenny, a COHSE nurse and the TASS lads mainly from Haverton Hill shipyard. I remember a trainload of us blocking the line at Aachen to prevent the German police taking off some of the delegation on some passport pretext. Also, hearing recently freed Angela Davis in the Stadium. My YCL 'Free Angela Davis' T-shirt was later worn to shreds.

Through the Middlesbrough branch of UNISON I arranged the first visit to the UK of a Bosnian trade union official. She was a senior nurse at Tuzla hospital. Her account, at a UNISON conference fringe-meeting, of the horrors of the war brought delegates to tears. I was later investigated for 'misuse of union funds' over this visit, but the officials eventually backed off.

Today my main effort is with the Palestine Solidarity Campaign and the Israeli Committee against House Demolitions UK, although I support Burma UK and Cuba Solidarity whenever I can. I have good friends in both Gaza and the West Bank who have stayed at our house. I feel as much passionate anger against imperialism today as I did when the issues were Vietnam and Chile.

I always hated the Eurocommunist label that some people tried to stick on me after the Commission on Inner-Party Democracy in 1977. It was a case of mistaken identity! I had agreed with the Majority Report except on the issue of the Political Committee, which in my experience always dominated the full Executive Committee. Reuben Falber, the Assistant General Secretary, lumped me in with the Minority Report as if I agreed with all of it. Nevertheless, I was fundamentally affected by identity politics, especially feminism. Reducing everything always and only to 'class' was – and remains – completely useless in terms of practical activity. We occasionally had a black man working at the depot – with all the usual kind of racist reactions. I felt I had a responsibility to deal with it. There was also an attempt to bring women in at one stage to do some road sweeping jobs. This really brought out the ugly and reactionary side of the working class. I never had any illusions about the working class. Rather, I was aware of what we had to overcome in order to unite all its many components and complex identities. People are always so much more complicated than a simple 'class' description allows for.

In 1988 I found myself press officer of the Campaign against Clause 28. I felt proud that so many gay and lesbian activists had confidence in me, despite my being heterosexual. It was only later that I was told that my chief qualification was that my union branch office at the time was on the fourth floor of Sun Alliance House. Out of range of bricks, of course!

In 1978-9 I was on the Party executive committee during the arguments between those who favoured Free Collective Bargaining and those who argued for a Statutory Incomes Policy. I was in neither camp. As a leading rank and file activist in NUPE, I was in favour of a Statutory Minimum Wage, but not curbs to reduce living standards. Most union leaders – and Bert Ramelson, the Party's Industrial Organiser – opposed the Statutory Minimum Wage as an interference in Free Collective Bargaining. Both sides were divorced from the low paid council workers who were about to explode into mass action. I was living day to day with these men and women and knew that no matter what union leaders or the Party wanted to happen, there was going to be action on a scale unprecedented since the end of the War. During the Winter of Discontent I was chair of the Cleveland Strike Committee of the NUPE/GMB/TGWU unions. The Strike Committee was in continuous session, seven days a week, 24 hours a day, for six weeks, with women being every bit as active on it as men. The Tees Valley was shut down tight due to our control of the winter gritting.

I have never regretted my role as the local leader of the strike. I saw the potential for working people to take control into their own hands. Many leading activists in years to come first emerged during the strike; at the same time, some useless time-servers were shown up for what they were. The energy, stamina and ingenuity of strike activists were inspiring. My own workplace, in keeping with its militant tradition, stayed out a seventh week when everybody else had returned to work. We won further pay concessions beyond what anybody else received. The bin-men were the Praetorian Guard of council workers!

Later in the same year there were the first directly elected European elections. The Party Executive agreed to stand a small number of candidates and I was endorsed for Cleveland as the CPGB candidate. The Political Committee saw fit to reverse this decision and not stand any candidates. But my campaign had already started rolling. My £500 or £600 candidate's deposit was provided by an interest-free loan from a sympathetic Co-op Bank manager. I stood as the 'Independent – For the Alternative Economic Strategy' candidate. I had a great time with public hustings, TV, Radio and Press interviews. I am afraid that my campaign ripped Labour's apart. I was supported by many trade unionists and Labour Party members. The Labour candidate was Ernest Wistrich, Director of the European Movement, the Liberals had a plummy grammar school head teacher from Scarborough and the Tories Peter Vanneck, a former Lord Mayor of London with a very slurry voice. During the campaign he offered me a drink from one of the two hip flasks he always carried. With my Methodist Sunday-School background I had to decline. I eventually received 4,960 votes.

I still miss the intellectual and campaigning comradeship of people working for a better world, people whom I liked and respected and from whom I drew strength in all sorts of ways. I made my small contribution, but in a movement where I felt I got back far more than I gave. Party membership gave me contact with deeply thinking people who came from widely different backgrounds – university lecturers, miners, dockers– there was such a mix. There were people involved in the peace movements, International Solidarity, the Co-op – such a tremendous variety – but the common denominator was being a member of the Communist Party.

I had a lot of respect for Beatrix Campbell. She was prepared to speak truths that others dared not even contemplate. And Dave Cook was a lovely bloke and a very important figure for me. I used to stay with Dave and his kids and various partners in London. It was always an experience; politics was much more important to Dave than housework. I often supported his politics but not on Internal Party

Democracy. Who else? Maria Loftus and Irene Swann, later on Joanna de Groot. Nina Temple and Ian McKay, Jack Ashton and Pete Carter. Pete played a prominent role in many different struggles. We were once involved in writing a pamphlet for the Party about the future of the trades union movement. When I raised the issue of internal union democracy I was jumped on from such a great height by Pete. This was absolutely taboo. We couldn't talk about it.

I don't miss the time and energy wasted on boring internalised meetings that went nowhere. And I don't miss the sectarianism. There were many in the Party with whom it was possible to have an open and honest disagreement. But there were always some with closed minds, who were not prepared to change as life itself demanded. The Party's close relationships with so many trade union leaders often compromised our politics. We were prepared to pretend that the anti-democratic abuses that were obvious to most people were not really an issue. Issues of internal union democracy were supposed to be a distraction from the class struggle. Of course, eventually, Thatcher took advantage of this weakness. In a sense the Coalition are still taking advantage of it. I believe that trade unions ought to be the shock troops of democracy. If you identify a problem you can talk about it; if you don't, it just gets worse.

EQUAL PAY

At the end of the 1960s there was a national dispute known as the dirty jobs strike involving bin-men, gardeners and road workers. We were on appallingly low wages. It was my first strike. I was only 19, but was asked by the Regional Officer, Keith Robinson, to help distribute strike pay in cash. It was a dangerous task carrying several thousand pounds. Even more dangerous was having to tell some huge binmen that they were not entitled to strike pay. At the time the Labour government had a Prices and Incomes Board, and the only way you could get an increase in pay was by increasing productivity. So NUPE, the T&G and the GMB signed up to increased productivity in return for substantial pay increases. The extra pay was produced through job losses. It was a trade-off. Workplaces like mine lost roughly a third of the workers. Part of the money saved went in the form of a bonus and part went to the employer. The only people with bonus schemes were men. Women were told they could not have them. They were already working so hard that there weren't any efficiency savings to be made (not that this stopped the employers from trying to increase the work load, especially in school kitchens). These productivity bonus schemes soon became an unacknowledged part of the men's wages, rapidly growing from 33 per cent of the basic wage to 50 per cent and 60 per cent. In Birmingham they reached 200%! Men were paid these 'productivity bonuses' even when on holiday or on the sick. The bonus for cutting grass, etc, was paid in winter as well as summer. What you had was very effective trade union representation – for men, by men and on behalf of men.

Meanwhile the Sex Discrimination and Equal Pay Acts were passed, in 1970. Employers were given five years to put their houses in order. The private sector 'put things right' by trying to reduce the wages of the men down to the level of the women. The local government trade unions knew that if they fought the issue the same thing was likely to happen to their male members. They avoided the issue of equal pay for women. Year after year of passing resolutions but doing nothing.

That was until 1996 and the Cleveland County Council dispute. This arose from a classic attempt by the employers to cut wages. Due to compulsory competitive tendering, the left Labour-controlled Cleveland County Council proposed to cut the wages of the women in the kitchens and the men on the ground-staff. The unions got the cuts withdrawn for the men, but not the women. A GMB Regional Officer, Eileen Goodenough, decided to make a real fight of it. She persuaded the GMB Regional Secretary to involve Thompson Solicitors and their leading employment lawyer Stefan Cross. He converted a legal dispute over an unfair deduction of wages into an equal pay dispute. He claimed between 30 per cent to 40 per cent increases in pay and pension entitlements to the level of the men. Eventually the women shared out £5 million between them.

UNISON did everything possible to prevent the case developing. The other three Teeside UNISON branches were prepared to sacrifice the women's claim, but, as secretary of the largest branch, I refused to go along with this. Eventually, fear that the GMB might pinch all our members caused the union to reluctantly authorise legal action. When the cases were won Unison quickly claimed the credit for it. The unions agreed that the women should have a 4 per cent bonus whilst the men still enjoyed 30-40 per cent – plus 'attendance' allowances.

Immediately after the success of the Cleveland case, a deal was struck to get rid of me. Middlesbrough Council and UNISON wanted to make sure that there were no more equal pay claims put in. Unison gave Middlesbrough Council the nod to sack me. The council began disciplinary action against me over a series of concocted charges. UNISON provided me with excellent legal representation, Stefan Cross again and Jenny Eadie, a brilliant barrister. But after I won my case for trade union victimisation at an employment tribunal, UNISON took a formal decision at the Northern Regional Council not to support my reinstatement. For me, this was more painful than being sacked. UNISON betrayed their fundamental duty to support a victimised activist. Only three principled people present opposed this: Jamshid Ahmad, Maureen Bickle and Eileen Tyson. Shameful.

The ex-NUPE activists had been virtually annihilated in the Northern Region. They were easy meat for more sophisticated white-collar, university-educated ex-NALGO people going under the banner of 'Unison Left'. Traditional opposition to equal pay claims in NUPE, GMB and the T&G came from the fear that the men's bonuses would be attacked (which could and did happen through Job Evaluation). But the opposition from NALGO was totally different – they didn't have bonuses to protect. Their fear was that job evaluation would upset their apple cart of established differentials. The different vested interests coincided. Some union activists refused to make an equal pay claim out of misplaced loyalty to the union, and some even tried to stop other women from doing so. We all like to think that the trade union movement always fights on behalf of working people. The reality in local government is they fought for a minority of men on bonus schemes, and so betrayed the interests of the great majority of union members – women cleaners, kitchen staff and carers. The trade union movement has never owned up to betraying the women. There has been no apology, or even acknowledgment, that the three major unions in local government did next to nothing over equal pay for years. Even now there are local councils where the battle is *still* going on, more than thirty-six years after the Equal Pay Act came into force.

In 2003 I started working with Stefan Cross, campaigning for equal pay for women workers in local government. After spending a few months working in Cumbria and driving around beautiful Cumbrian countryside, it was agreed that I should work on my old turf in Middlesbrough. Suddenly, the situation exploded, with meetings of up to 600 women. We spent next to nothing on publicity. It was through the women's' networks that the campaign had taken off. There is a trail through sisters, friends, neighbours, mothers and daughters across the North East, in Middlesbrough, Redcar, Stockton and Hartlepool, to Sunderland and Newcastle and back to Durham. We thought our campaign would be a catalyst, forcing the unions to join in. But we were very wrong. The unions reacted in the most defensive and hostile way imaginable. They worked with the employers to deny their own members their legal entitlements.

I also worked in South Yorkshire and Wales. The Rotherham meetings at the Silverdale Miners Welfare were amongst my most enjoyable. Large meetings of working-class women, full of laughs as well as serious commitment to their entitlements; packed meetings in women's living rooms and kitchens where I was grilled to make sure that what I was saying made sense. Some meetings were tough, especially when putting out leaflets outside the 'Briefings' organised jointly by employers and unions to get the women to sign away their rights for a pittance. I was slapped in the face by a female council official in Bishop Auckland and thumped by a union official outside Newcastle Civic Centre. Meetings were disrupted in Sunderland and Llanelli, and the women often faced abusive pickets from their union, trying to stop them from coming in to hear me. The Llanelli meeting had the biggest impact on me. Three women had been let down by UNISON and were very angry. They had got nothing from Equal Pay because their union had failed to tell them their rights. They had all retired on health grounds, including one who had breast cancer. Though Stefan Cross could do nothing to help then, I promised that I would not forget their situation and would try to get justice for them. This will need a change in the law, or a government that is prepared to accept their moral obligation to pay all women cheated since 1975. I still want to campaign for this. The 1997 Labour government acted to compensate miners and their families for work-related ill-health from the date that the mines were nationalised. I think that giving women the money and higher pensions owed to them since 1975 would be a better way of boosting the economy than the Quantitative Easing favoured by the Bank of England.

DEMOCRATIC LEFT

In the Party's last years I thought the game was up. There was no point in attempting to stagger on. Activity and membership were collapsing. I thought we had to do something different. But, like lots of other people, I didn't know what. I saw Democratic Left as a way of getting to a position where we could regroup and try to develop something different. I never saw it as a permanent organisation. It was too tiny. I saw it as a way of salvaging something out of the wreck of the Party.

I played an active part in establishing the DL constitution. I was a Council member as well as a director and shareholder of Rodell Properties where the assets of the Party ended up. I am still a director and shareholder, but hope to pass this responsibility on soon. DL adopted many very progressive ideas. By coincidence, I was involved in the creation of UNISON and Democratic Left at the same time, as I was a nationally elected leader of both. The 'Values' section of UNISON's rule book is almost a direct lift from the constitution of Democratic Left.

Democratic Left had some important successes such as launching Unions 21. It concentrated more and more on democratic issues and gave up any pretensions to being a Party, or even wanting to establish a new one. It needed to move on and change further otherwise it would have collapsed.

I was chair of the New Times Network, the New Politics Network and then of Unlock Democracy. NPN had rescued Charter 88 from financial collapse. Eventually the membership of both organisations agreed to a complete merger, thereby creating a new and stronger campaigning organisation for democratic advance. In the last elections to the Unlock Democracy Council I faced four Parliamentary candidates and national officials of the Liberal Democrat Party, and came fifth in a constituency that returned four council members.

Since two of them failed to attend meetings, however, I am now back on, hopefully older and wiser.

LABOUR PARTY

1989 till 1993 were really bad years for me. I lost the anchors of my Party, my union and my relationship. I went into serious depression.

I joined the Labour Party in Middlesbrough in 1994. Shortly afterwards, I moved to Darlington. The Labour party in Darlington was very interesting. Alan Milburn was regarded as a leading Blairite. He ran Darlington as a Stalinist fiefdom. Anyone who differed from him was crushed and excluded, absolutely and ruthlessly. I worked with other people to develop a decent branch, in the West End. We were increasing attendance, membership and activity. The Milburn machine, mainly councillors, swamped the AGM and replaced all the people who had been doing the work. They destroyed the branch. They were much happier with a dead branch.

When I moved to North Tyneside, in late 2008, I joined the North Tyneside Constituency Labour Party and the Benton Branch. In 2009 I stood in the local council elections, in Weetslade and came within 200 votes of winning. At the next election somebody else was picked as the candidate there and I was asked to stand in Benton. The branch had slowly collapsed over the years. It was dead. Working with John, in his eighties, and Janet, an ex-councillor, my partner and I started to bring the branch back to life. The branch is now approaching a hundred members. We are by far the biggest and most active branch in North Tyneside. We had fifty people active in the last election campaign. In May 2010, I defeated one of the three Tory councillors. In 2011, we defeated another Tory, a cabinet member. Only one more to go, in 2012.

I look on being a councillor the same as when I was a shop steward. Only, instead of a workplace, I represent a geographical area. The problems and people are more diverse and the challenges greater. Homelessness, poverty, the local environment, the cuts, all bring people to my door. Making a difference is still possible. But to deal with the bigger problems will still require a change of government and society.

My experience in North Tyneside was being picked as the council candidate by the long-serving CLP secretary rather than by a democratically convened ward meeting. When the local government committee was re-established, after many years without one, I was elected secretary. The 'old guard' didn't like this one little bit. Sitting councillors, previously, had not had to be interviewed to stand again, because, once you were a councillor, you were a councillor for life. I followed the Labour Party rule-book and we went through the full process of interviewing all the candidates for the panel. None of them were deselected – but the impertinence of making them face an interview!

After I became a councillor I was elected an assistant whip. The junior positions had not been stitched up. I had been assistant whip for only a week when I was approached by a woman councillor. She told me that she had been bullied and harassed by certain senior members of the Labour group for four years. Eventually I felt I had no choice but to take the issue to the National Party, at the 2010 Conference in Manchester. Within days I was threatened with disciplinary action; shortly afterwards my membership was suspended by the General Secretary of the Labour Party on behalf of the NEC. I have since been removed from all the Labour Party elected positions I held and from every position on the council that I could legally be removed from. Over a year later I remain suspended. I have had a single interview of a little over an hour. There is no time limit on suspensions in the Labour Party. It is a good job that I have a sense of humour and a knowledge of Kafka.

The Refounding Labour document seems positive to me in trying to describe the problems facing the Labour Party. However, if Ed Miliband and Peter Hain want to change things they are going to have to tackle the Blairite legacy. The machinery hasn't changed. The officials are largely the same ones who were there under Blair and Brown. Perhaps the new General Secretary will make a difference.

Given my situation, I thought it wise not to attend this year's Labour Party Conference in Liverpool. But I wrote and printed a Labour Campaign for Electoral Reform leaflet distributed at the conference, sounding the alarm about the Coalition's plans for 'Individual Voter Registration', which could mean 10 million people losing their votes.

I am sixty-one now. I will be a councillor for the next two years before making way for a newer person. We have a lot of very good people in the Benton Branch. The North Tyneside CLP has had all-member CLP meetings, which means that every member living in the constituency is entitled to attend CLP meetings and to vote. When lots of people turned up at the last AGM, the Chair announced that only delegates were eligible to vote. Apparently, the regional officer of the Labour Party had just discovered (the night before!) that the constituency had never formally asked for permission to become an all-member constituency, six years previously. Our branch is still waiting for the constituency secretary to tell us if, and when, the constituency is going to apply for all-member status. The last time he was asked he replied that the situation is 'still as it was'.

The Party is dead, long live the party!

Dave Cope

Activism is my rent for living on this planet
Alice Walker

LIVERPOOL

I was born in 1951 into a Communist family in Liverpool. Both parents were teachers and it was always my mother who was the more active and committed – my father admitted only to selling the *Daily Worker* on the Dock Road after the war as part of his courting strategy, and after my mother's death he joined the Labour Party. My younger brother, Robin, joined the YCL, CPGB, Democratic Left and Labour Party in that order.

One of my first political memories is of regular visits by the Literature Secretary. This role will be familiar to many readers – but a mystery to most British people. Frank Parkinson came round every Friday with his pile of publications, and more importantly a pack of Fox's Glacier Mints, which he immediately presented to me. Frank's bribery worked better than he ever could have imagined – I developed an obsession with left-wing literature that still dominates my life.

I never joined the YCL – it *was* the 1960s and you had to rebel against something, so I rebelled against what I considered my parents' lack of political activity by this time. I finally joined the CP at university in 1971. I went through the motions of checking out the other left organisations, but it was inevitable I would end up in the CP. It was the quality of the CP's active members, their selflessness and political intelligence, and the Party's working-class links that convinced me. I soon found my place as Lit Sec. I recall one unfortunate rainy evening after a bookstall at a meeting, when we went for a long session in the pub to celebrate a victory (or was it to seek consolation for a defeat?), and on the way home I stumbled so that many of the unsold books and pamphlets ended up soggy and soiled. Fortunately nobody used this mishap to usurp me from my position.

In 1975 I was back in Liverpool, and the CP decided to move its bookshop, Progressive Books, to proper shop premises. I was working in a library and active in the Party, and was offered the job as manager; there would be volunteers to help in the shop, and a bookshop committee would be set up to help run it. The job was correctly seen as a political one, and I was then invited to attend meetings of the Merseyside Area committee, to which I was later elected. This was a subcommittee of the North West District committee, and while very important for co-ordinating the work of the fifty CP branches on Merseyside, it did not have the constitutional role of a District, though we had more members than some Districts.

This was the golden era of radical bookshops. In Liverpool alone there were several – there was an anarchist/feminist one, and a short-lived shop opened by the International Socialists on the same block in the same week as us. Soon the WRP and the CPB(ML) opened up shops – the former was characterised by the revolutionary concept of hiding the works of Marx and Trotsky behind books of local interest and Mills & Boon, while the latter was part of a small franchise specialising in Maoist memorabilia. Choice was the name of the game. The Labour Party alone did not have a bookshop. The communist movement had an unquenchable belief in the written word – a common feature of the Labour movement that predated, and is not exclusive to, communism – but the CPGB produced an astonishing amount of material and an infrastructure to distribute it that was unique – more like that of a mass party.

At Progressive Books we developed links with local trade unions, trades councils, Labour Party branches, WEA classes and student organisations, and we provided many bookstalls. I am sure we sold more copies of Tressell's *The Ragged Trousered Philanthropists* than any other shop in the country – at least 3000 paperbacks and 500 hardbacks in the time I was there.

It was through *The Ragged Trousered Philanthropists* that I met my future wife. In 1977 there was a programme of events to commemorate the erection of a gravestone to Tressell, who died in Liverpool and had been buried in an unmarked pauper's grave, and we flyposted adverts for the book and the bookshop all over the city centre. Leena, a Finnish young communist working in Liverpool, saw the poster and discovered the bookshop and me. Perhaps a short digression on personal relationships within the CPGB can be permitted here. During my twenty-year membership of the Party all three of my serious relationships were with party members. Whether this is of any statistical value, or indeed interest, I have no idea – but it does indicate the 'alternative community' function that the CP could fulfil.

Slightly socially conservative the CP may have been – though much less so by the 1970s – but there was certainly no class snobbery. It was one of the great qualities of the CP that people of all backgrounds worked together unselfconsciously. One of Merseyside's most articulate and well-read members was Jack Kay, a building worker who married a university lecturer. Of course, articulate middle-class members had an advantage at meetings and debates, and some working-class members might initially feel a bit reticent about speaking up; but working-class members were actively encouraged to take up positions of responsibility – positive discrimination before the term was coined. Membership of the CP, with its encouragement of discussion, reading, debate, and attention to cultural affairs, was an education of a life-enhancing nature for many working-class activists. Was there any inverse snobbery, any middle-class pandering to workers? Yes, occasionally, but such awkwardness or falseness in discourse was soon apparent. Were there examples of workerism, did any members play the working-class card? Yes, of course, and in some cases this was harder to dislodge, especially if expressed by leading trade unionists. In general, my experience was that there was respect for the individual skills and contributions of each member.

We took a very broad approach to what we stocked in the shop, not being averse to controversy. Trotskyism, Maoism, anarchism – we stocked it all, even the Spartacists' material. There was some controversy over *Straight Left* during the period of the final split, as the contributors were a faction in the CP and didn't write under their real names, but we still stocked it.

After the first few years of our existence, when radical, feminist and socialist books could only be found in radical bookshops, the major chains joined in the action and this seriously affected the viability of our shop and others like it. It was difficult to survive just from selling books so we developed the non-book side of the business – stationery, posters, local framed photographs – and we got into badges very early in the craze. We purchased a badge machine and made our own. We developed quite an imaginative entrepreneurial approach – perhaps a bit too imaginative in a couple of cases involving stock offered by some dodgy characters. We also started selling second-hand books donated by members. Apart from myself, in the shop's heyday there was a part-time worker on four days a week, and plenty of volunteers who also helped out. Our Monday volunteer was John Gibson, a stalwart of the British Soviet Friendship Society, and on that day the shop became like a branch of the Novosti Press Agency.

LONDON

I separated from my wife, who died shortly afterwards in sad circumstances, largely due to the effects of alcoholism. Needing a change of environment, in 1987 I moved to London to work for Central Books, the Communist Party's book distributor, which also ran a shop. I moved into a house in Hackney belonging to a group of comrades, one of whom was Bill Norris, the manager of Central Books.

I worked in the shop in Grays Inn Road, soon taking responsibility for the second-hand department. I later moved to the warehouse in Southwark to help with the accounts department while still working one day a week in the shop organising the second-hand books. The warehouse moved to Hackney Wick in 1990 and the shop was closed in 1992, a victim of the decline of independent bookshops, the radical book trade and the demise of the CP. The ownership of both Lawrence & Wishart and Central Books was transferred from Democratic Left to their management and staff. In the case of Central, shares were distributed on the basis of a combination of management responsibility and time worked there. The aim was to maintain the political identity of the businesses, and it was a very successful project. Much of this is covered in my little book *Central Books: A Brief History, 1939-1999*. As well as being a narrative account, this explored various themes such as the relationship between politics and business, staff relations, and the radical book trade. So I won't say more here.

When we closed the shop, I bought the remaining stock of second-hand books and set up Left on the Shelf as a mail order business. I worked four days a week for Central and the rest of the time on my small but growing second-hand book business. My work at Central changed over the years – I worked as credit controller, juggler of payments to publishers and for the last couple of years as personnel manager – and I think I introduced some good practices. I was Company Secretary from 1988 till I left, and am still a Director.

We had active Party branches in Hackney, but this was the endgame for the CP, and divisions were bitter. Public activity declined as some joined the Communist Campaign Group and then the CPB; others gradually dropped out of activity, even if they were in political sympathy with the leadership. Personal relationships became strained. It was possible to be polite to the 'opposition' up to a point, as long as one didn't talk about the differences, but soon even this became difficult. Most of my circle of friends in Liverpool and Hackney and co-workers at Central were on the Eurocommunist wing, supportive of the leadership and outraged at what we saw as the hijacking of the *Morning Star* and organised factionalism. We were slow to respond in kind and only reluctantly accepted the necessity of administrative measures. Obviously, for several years there had been organised jockeying on both sides at the joint branch meetings to get their candidates elected to Congresses. I went to a couple of Congresses while still in Liverpool, and then the final one in 1991 that saw the transformation to Democratic Left, which I voted for.

ASSESSMENT

By the end of its existence, the CP was, unfortunately, irrelevant. It had played a huge role in my life. There were a few eccentrics, there were more bores, but I made many friends – even now, on returning to Liverpool I am pleased to catch up with old comrades from whatever faction. I've got the CP to thank for my career – not many people can say that. In fact more were blacklisted for being Communists than benefitted materially from membership.

In the eyes of the public we were, not unnaturally, identified with the Soviet Union – we were a small franchise of a larger brand that was not particularly popular. In the Party there were more than two views of the Soviet Union, and more than two views of what the Party should become. However, as a broad generalisation, pro-Soviet views went with a traditional view of Marxism-Leninism. I was always very sceptical about Leninism. I could admire Lenin as a great revolutionary tactician, and as leader of a revolution where one wasn't expected to happen, and someone who had worked to sustain the revolution in incredibly adverse conditions. But for me this did not mean being a 'Leninist'. And I also don't feel the need to define myself as a Marxist. Marxism is a method of analysis; it is only a belief system in the broadest sense of expecting a socialist future to develop from capitalism. Marx and Engels spent little time writing about the socialist revolution or the future socialist society they predicted. It was later communists who created a rigid theory of revolution they termed Marxism-Leninism, believing the revolution and the revolutionary Party were to follow the pattern of those of Lenin. And in this process a lot of the native socialist tradition in Britain –as in other countries – was forgotten. Marx disliked the term Marxism, and Lenin that of Marxism-Leninism, but that was the new orthodoxy.

By its end the CP consisted of several communist parties, but perhaps it was predominantly a libertarian body – it was certainly liberal in the best sense of the word. This may sound surprising or shocking, but consider this: its constitution had become unreal; its medium-term programme utopian (even the hope of a left Labour government with a few Communist MPs); class was no longer regarded as the sole defining function in politics (the CP had championed feminism and a rich cultural politics); Lenin was seen as irrelevant; and the party did not advocate any existing model of socialism. It debated with the centre of British politics and not just the left; and it was critical of certain trade union practices. Just reflect on how much the Party had changed between 1920 to 1951, when the first edition of the *British Road to Socialism* appeared, and then on the changes in the following forty years. Different world, different problems, different solutions.

I know some people can't accept the possibility of there being no need for 'the revolutionary party', but I had no problem with that. Even Marx was prepared to see the demise of the International Workingmen's Association rather than see it fall into the hands of the Bakuninists (and the IWMA was the revolutionary party of Marx's day, which he had nurtured from birth). Events will throw up the leaders and organisations that are required.

Organisationally, the CP was an anachronism. Built originally on the model of the Bolshevik party, it was top heavy, with a largely self-perpetuating leadership; full-time workers spent too much time just maintaining the organisation. Meetings became formulaic: at our Merseyside Area committee we had to listen to a Political Report by our Chairman, which was a repeat of the report originally given at the EC, and that he or another comrade from the EC had already given to the District Committee (and which the members of the AC who were also on the DC would already have heard). We were supposed to pass on the substance of this report, and most importantly its decisions, to our branches. All this would have been filtered by the Secretariats of the DC, then the AC, then the Branch committee. For a small organisation this was madness.

What distinguished the Communist Party in Britain was the quality of its activists; its selflessness in working with other organisations (though perhaps some elements of control remained in trade union work); its internationalism; its optimism that socialism could be renewed, that changes could happen even under capitalism; that debate and the printed word were important – and yes, a sense of discipline. It could set the intellectual agenda on occasions, as it did through *Marxism Today* and the Communist Universities. Although the CPGB's stated aim of achieving a working-class revolution was not achieved, and was not on the horizon, its work was not necessarily a failure. But by the 1990s it had outlived its time: a name change would not have been enough, the world was changing, and communism as practised in the twentieth century was a failed project.

So what was the legacy of the CP? I think we can dismiss the New Communist Party, 1977 vintage. The Communist Party of Britain has a better claim as the successor organisation: though strictly speaking the successor was Democratic Left, we can't ignore the CPB, especially as the *Morning Star* is still appearing and is undeniably better than it was under Tony Chater and the CPGB – it is bigger, more colourful and open to a broader range of opinions. The survival of this part of the legacy is pretty astonishing, especially as it is also available for free online. It was a few years before I could look at the paper again after the split, and then a few more before I started reading it regularly. It still infuriates me on occasions: the readers' letters can be prejudiced and sectarian, and there are always supporters of Gaddafi, North Korea, Irish Republican terrorism, Mugabe and the like. It is at its worst in dealing with the CPGB – when Gordon McLennan died the paper had some very unpleasant articles and letters. And the paper does get its knickers in a twist over the Labour Party: it wants to appeal to the 'Labour Left', and carries articles by Corbyn and Livingstone, but it also possesses an irrepressible urge to attack the leadership, sometimes with vicious or petty personal attacks. This was a perennial problem for the CPGB too: support the Labour Party or not, apply to join or not, stand candidates against it or not, differentiate between party and government or not.

There are other ways one can trace the legacy of the CPGB. I've already referred to Central Books and Lawrence & Wishart, and for all their limitations (for instance, Central never became the natural home of the larger left-wing publishers such as Pluto or Zed, and L&W's limited resources meant it did not attract many major new writers) they should not be underestimated for providing a home to authors and publishers who would not otherwise have been published or distributed. And the politics of many of these authors and publishers continued the spirit of debate and the pluralism that the CPGB encouraged. Similarly, the Marx Memorial Library and the Working Class Movement Library, while never having belonged to the Party, were created within its tradition by party members, and both thrive to this day. The intellectual legacy also continues in the Socialist History Society (a direct successor to the influential CP Historians' Group) and its publications. And such work is only a small part of the wide-ranging project to record and analyse the history of the CPGB. Since 1991 there has been a veritable avalanche of material produced about the Party, and this book will not be the last. These range from oral history projects, to journals, conferences, self-published autobiographies (inevitably of varying quality), and dozens of academic studies. My online bibliography of the CPGB is another manifestation of this interest.

This said, the legacy is disappointing and somewhat puzzling. Where one might have expected a major impact is in the Labour Party – if enough ex-members had joined – but this by and large has not happened. This is in spite of the influence of *Marxism Today* and the CP on the debate about the renewal of the Labour Party under Kinnock and after, including in the development of New Labour, which has been much commented upon. However, many of those who might have joined were fed up with internal struggles and wanted a break from organised party politics. The struggle for electoral victory prior to 1997 would have benefited from the input of ex-Communists.

Many leading Communists had been asked to join the Labour Party over the preceding forty years, and been told unofficially that they would be supported if they stood in local or national elections. Few did this, however, and few who were still members in 1991 thought of following this route. Liverpool and Hackney, the areas where I had been active, both had a relatively strong CP, but they show very few members joining the Labour Party, let alone gaining leading positions: one member became a councillor in Liverpool but none did in Hackney. Further research on this would be interesting. There is a small group of ex-CPers who are prominent in Unite, but otherwise there is little evidence of the CP in the trade union movement.

The other, less tangible, area of CP influence is in a way of working in other organisations. Communists certainly joined and were elected to leading positions in many other groups: contrary to the common perception, they did not do this to further the aims of the Party by recruiting members (in fact we were often criticised within the Party for *not* doing enough to recruit them), but because such work was part of our world outlook as communists. This differentiated our approach from that of the Trotskyists, who would use other organisations primarily to build their own. No doubt many former members continued to work in this way, and others put more effort into these organisations than previously; some must have joined new ones, but I'm not sure this amounted to much that can be measured.

THE PARTY IS DEAD – LONG LIVE THE PARTY!

My memory of Democratic Left is actually quite hazy. It was a relief to be rid of the unproductive fighting with those who were supposed to be on the same side – family arguments are always the worst. And it was a relief to be working with those of similar views, even if disappointing that so few joined. There were not the same pressures of activity and regular branch and district meetings. It soon became apparent that the original intentions were too ambitious,; DL was more like a large progressive think tank – which was not such a bad thing to be. I enjoyed the paper *New Times*. I have the memory of finding it quite difficult to know what we should be doing, and that it was surprisingly hard to get out of the old CP mindset and formalities. I went along with DL till it changed into the New Politics Network. I didn't follow the details of what subsequently happened, but it seems a pity that the financial legacy disappeared so quickly and unproductively.

After this I enjoyed a period of being politically promiscuous: I voted Labour or Green depending on the election. I had a holiday from organised politics and concentrated on work at Central Books and building up Left on the Shelf, both of which for me had a strong political element. My partner, Ginny, whom I had met in 1993, moved in with me when she downsized on leaving a well-paid job in the upper echelons of UNISON. Ginny had been a member of the Labour Party for years – having been involved in the GLC's Women's Committee she was recruited by Ken Livingstone, who argued the need to bring feminist politics into the Labour Party. So she had entered the Labour Party with the hope of introducing new ideas and ways of working. I joined in 2000. There were various factors. One was her influence; another was that I wanted to understand why Hackney was in such a mess (I wanted to get involved in local politics and do something positive to make it a better place to live in); another was that I missed political discussion and involvement – I felt that my holiday had lasted long enough. Entryism it was not. By this time the first flush of enthusiasm of Blair's election had worn off, and to some it may appear a strange time to have joined. Our MP, Diane Abbott, remarked on this when I met her at a Labour Party house party. But that didn't dissuade me – I had experience in a declining political party. I had never been cynical about the Labour Party, and I'd known a lot of good, mainly left-wing members. I'd been critical of Labour's electoralism – I wanted a political party to have a wider function – but I'd always recognised the importance of elections; if you couldn't persuade people to vote for you how could you expect them to follow you to the barricades? I always rejoiced in Labour's electoral victories over the Tories, for whom I retain a visceral antipathy. I always felt scorn for the argument that the workers needed a dose of right wing politics before they would turn to socialism, and despite Labour's failures and weaknesses I felt the argument that all the parties were the same (pro-capitalist) was simplistic and somewhat arrogant.

I'd even accepted Tony Blair's removal of Clause 4 – emotionally appealing though it was, it was in the language of another era. It was the Labour Party's equivalent of Marxism-Leninism. And to those who snort in disgust at such reformism, I say go and re-read the replacement clause in Labour's constitution: it's pretty good. A brief comment about Blair here: Labour would not have won those three victories without him; or if it could have won in 1997 – given the widespread desire for change – the victory would not have been as great or long-lasting. Blair was both Labour's greatest asset and its greatest liability.

You might be aware by now that I'm not one for quoting Lenin, but one of my favourites is 'The truth is revolutionary'; and the truth, as it appears to me, is that socialist revolution is not on the agenda. This may be regrettable, but what is on the agenda is – for example – the need to retain the civil liberties we've won, and the steps we've won towards an end to discrimination based on gender, race and sexual orientation, as well, in the short term, as the defence of the NHS and social fabric of the country, through defeating the Tories and their Lib-Dem stooges. The achievements that we have made and need to defend were won by action outside and inside Parliament: without the Labour Party they would not have happened. It's up to each of us to do what we can, and the Labour Party has a key role in this. Voting Labour is not the only thing we can do, but it's a necessary thing.

At the same time, we should be arguing for a change in economic policy – for a greater burden to be placed on those who can afford to pay, for tighter control of financial institutions, for greener solutions and for an ethical foreign policy. My politics involves fighting for immediate winnable goals but always having a wider perspective to aim at; in that sense, socialism is the agenda.

Of course, there have been issues where the Labour government has tended to be part of the problem rather than the solution, and every member will have had their reason to consider leaving: Iraq of course, faith schools, PFIs, erosion of civil liberties, pandering to America, pandering to Murdoch, pandering to bankers and so on. But the Labour Party, like all others, is only what its members make of it, and these weaknesses can be and have been reversed, even if only partially so far. And the list of Labour's achievements is longer – the minimum wage, the money put into hospitals and schools, the right to roam, devolution, tax policies for families, Sure Start, the 0.7 per cent of GDP allocated to international development, etc. One could easily add to both these lists.

In Hackney, Labour transformed itself and turned round a failing borough. It had to take some unpleasant decisions initially to maintain a legal budget, but it explained the issues to the electorate and won them over. The non-Labour left has always been very weak on local politics, and this had always frustrated me. I played an active role in the party in Hackney, in my ward branch and on the General Committee. It was a pleasure to participate in some superbly organised election campaigns – and it is such a satisfying feeling to win an election.

I sometimes wondered if the role of the main political parties was more and more limited, or even if their era was nearing an end. But though there has been a growth of one-issue movements, and of organisations based on the net or social networks, and new organisations like UKUncut, none of this has yet led me to believe the role of the Labour Party is over. These are all fascinating developments and I am excited by several of them, but the Labour Party still has a key role in electoral politics, and can work with these movements if it is imaginative enough. In the immediate term the Labour Party is still essential. I cannot foresee the creation of a political party – even if there was a merger of some existing parties and organisations – that would tempt me away from the Labour Party. The extra-parliamentary left has a dismal history of splits and sectarianism and shows no sign of changing. Maybe I've learned the need for long-term commitment and stubbornness from my time in the CP. But I recognise the dilemmas and options open to socialists and activists looking for a home – especially in some areas where Labour has a deadening monopoly of control and unimaginative leadership; and in Scotland there is the attraction of the SNP, and elsewhere the pull of a strong Green Party. I remain open to different possibilities for activity in the future.

By the time we left Hackney, Labour had a massive majority on the council – though of course we can only claim the smallest of parts in this. The Lib-Dems had no seats (a couple of their councillors had been imprisoned for electoral misdemeanours), and the Tories were limited to a few seats in their stronghold in the Orthodox Jewish areas.

KENDAL

We'd decided a few years earlier that we wanted to move to Kendal, a market-town large enough to have a good social, cultural and political life – but close to the hills. The internet made it just possible to make a basic living from Left on the Shelf, and Ginny was also self-employed and could work from anywhere with reasonable transport links – we'd decided we wanted to try to manage without buying a car.

One of the first things I did in Kendal was to get involved in an organisation outside the LP. I'd been a paper member of the World Development Movement for a couple of years, and when the local group advertised a public meeting in the Town Hall shortly after our arrival in Kendal, I went along, had a chat in the pub afterwards and that was it: the right organisation, the right people, at the right time. That's how political involvement can happen. After a couple of years I became secretary and one of the mainstays of the organisation in the area, together with a good group of committed activists. I did want to work in an organisation less formal than the LP or CP, more open to imaginative ways of working and simply more enjoyable – and younger. WDM has a network of over fifty autonomous local groups within a democratic structure, serviced by an enthusiastic head office which houses a formidable research and lobbying organisation of national and international significance. It works with campaigning NGOs from the global south, and British organisations working on similar issues – Oxfam, Greenpeace, People and Planet, etc. It has been in existence for over forty years, it helped set up the Fair Trade Foundation, and it is part of the Jubilee Debt Campaign. Its key slogan is Justice for the World's Poor, and it believes the main obstacles to this are multinational companies and free market economics. Marx would have approved of this emphasis on the primacy given to an economic analysis. Check us out.

In Kendal during the Make Poverty History campaign in 2005, we delivered over 10,000 leaflets in the 'Vote for Trade Justice' project, obtaining nearly 1,900 returns; we sent two coach loads to the Edinburgh G8 demo, including our MP and local bishop. We organise regular Schools Conferences for sixth formers; we hold the best local hustings of candidates in general and European elections. In February 2007 we held a public meeting on climate change (the first of its kind locally), with a Green activist from El Salvador, and 150 people attended; as a consequence we were able to set up a local campaign on climate change which has become a large and wide-ranging organisation. We've campaigned on RBS involvement in Canadian tar sands extraction – with black, oily footprints leading to the local branch. I could go on, but I think the variety of activity speaks for itself.

Kendal was, as expected, a completely different environment from inner city Liverpool and Hackney, which had been my homes for over twenty-five years. The social make-up and demographics for starters: a lot of retired people (many of whom were politically active), few young activists, a larger middle class, very little ethnic diversity. There was one CPB member, a Trotskyist, an anarchist and others including ex-LP members – and we all got on well, especially working against the BNP when they tried to show their face. I found myself working with a lot of committed Christians – Kendal being a centre of Quakerism, non-conformism and generally progressive religious people. They are much easier to work with than the far left – less sectarian, fewer hidden agendas, more willing to work collectively for a common cause. It must be said in passing that the fall of communism had led to an interesting softening of attitudes on the British and European far left since 1990.

Being in the Labour Party in Kendal is a bit like being in a revolutionary sect – Labour is the new Maoism here: we are treated with a mixture of horror and curiosity. Our vote in the last general election was the lowest in the country, despite a good candidate. The Westmorland and Lonsdale constituency had been a safe Tory seat from the early twentieth century, until in 2005 Tim Farron (currently President of the Lib-Dems, and on the left of the party) won the seat with a majority of 267, which he then turned into a fortress in the 2010 election, where he had a majority of nearly 12,300. A lot of Labour supporters, and even the occasional member, voted for Farron in 2005, to help remove the obnoxious Tim Collins, a shadow cabinet member and on the far right of the Tory Party. This tactical voting was repeated in 2010: the Lib-Dems cleverly played the 'help us retain this marginal seat' line, when in fact it should have been clear to all that Farron was going to win with a large majority.

The Lib-Dem machine then mopped up the Kendal Labour councillors on the town, District and County councils, with their usual combination of very localised street politics and gross opportunism. The Lib-Dems' ascendancy was achieved on the back of their extremely hard-working MP, and by 2010, they held all 28 town council seats. Some excellent councillors ended up losing their seats, generally to nobodies, which not surprisingly led to a period of despondency. Now not only is Kendal a one-party town, it also manifests a syndrome usually associated with totalitarian states: they fear losing the smallest bit of power in case it means the beginning of the end of all their power.

As in many parts of the country, Labour activists in local politics often dislike the Lib-Dems more than the Tories: the argument is that you know where you stand with the latter, who are more honest. But I have never been a councillor, nor wanted to be one; my politics are more driven by national, and perhaps even international, considerations. To me the Tories are the real enemy – the class enemy and the major threat to civil liberties and progressive politics in general, at home and abroad. I am as keen as anyone to see more Labour representation in our area, but sometimes find myself arguing that some Lib-Dem policies nationally over the last few years have been more progressive than Labour's. Not only this, but it's not impossible that Labour will be negotiating with Tim Farron if there's another hung Parliament in the future.

At least Labour membership and activity in Westmorland has picked up since the defeat of 2010, and with the subsequent election of Ed Miliband as leader. We are facing the future with more optimism. Many of the highly political electors here who voted tactically will never do so again after the Lib-Dem coalition with the Tories. Over the last few years, our Labour Party has tried to broaden its appeal, and engage in a slightly different form of politics, and has held public meetings on subjects that are not typical Labour territory. We have simplified our structures, and reduced formalities at meetings while increasing the time for political discussion. Perhaps we have been left to our own devices by the regional organisation as we are of minimal importance in electoral terms, but there is a willingness under the new leadership to think outside the box, and I expect there will be even more flexibility and creative thinking in the area of organisation and politics.

As well as these changes we have had an interesting series of public meetings. There was one with survivors of the *Mavi Mamara*, organised in conjunction with the Palestine Solidarity Campaign. We've had a meeting on the cuts and another on the NHS, where we've worked with local unions, and we have tried to encourage campaigns to be set up. And most ambitiously in 2011 we organised a year-long series of cultural events to celebrate the ninetieth anniversary of the constituency. These included a guided walk on 'The Other Kendal', a concert with Leon Rosselson, a poetry reading (with Andy Croft), and talks on *The Ragged Trousered Philanthropists* and Theodora Wilson Wilson, a little known Kendal novelist, suffragist and pacifist. We also had a workshop based on material we are gathering for a book that Lord David Clark, a local labour historian, is writing about the history of the Labour Party and wider movement in

Westmorland. And we have produced some very high quality publicity material for all this.

I am very pleased that many of the speakers or performers at these and other events have not only been non-members, but also, to varying degrees, have been critical of the LP. This is a bit uncommon, but very healthy in my view; it does indicate a concept of the party as a facilitator or focus for the wider community of activists, and not just as an electoral machine (and we're not even an electoral machine in Kendal!) Some of these events have been well attended, others less so – there is still some distrust of the LP as well as a lot of downright hostility, and not all members are interested in, for example, poetry readings. And not all campaigns have taken off from some meetings as we might have hoped. But generally those attending have been impressed, and perhaps can begin to see the party in a new light. And these activities to some extent reflect my politics learned in the CP: the cultural events and Palestine meeting were my suggestions. I say this not to blow my own trumpet but to point out the possibilities within the Labour Party for this kind of politics, a perspective that may surprise readers. This is the evidence for my statement that all parties are what members make of them. Political organisations must allow space for the kind of activity members really want to engage in, not just what the organisation has done traditionally. So we should see greater variety in forms of activity on the left, depending on the skills and interests of members.

On the subject of members, there are two other areas of comparison between the CP and LP I would briefly like to discuss. I have always been more active at branch level, though also sometimes taking positions at the next level up (Area Committee in the CP, GC/EC in the LP); this is a reflection of my skills and interests. Similarly with WDM, my priority is to help maintain the local group. Without the basic membership unit in an organisation all else will fail. Of course, policy and national structures are important, but these are not my priorities. And in all the books and articles about political parties, these details about branch meetings, activities and social life are what slip through the gaps – yet this is what dominates most members' experience and perception of their organisation.

The first observation concerns active memberships. Most organisations have active and paper, or subscription (I dislike the term passive), members. The CPGB had a surprisingly large number of paper members, but it had a higher proportion of active ones than the Labour Party. Anyone who has been a member of the CP or LP will sometimes know the feeling of despair in trying to mobilise members. Our Westmorland CLP has a higher than average number of older members – some of whom are still very active. In Hackney there were more young activists at all levels, partly because this reflected the local population, but also because the LP held power and could achieve more and offered the potential of a political career. But age is not the only factor in non-activity; sometimes people think the act of joining itself is enough for them – and it can certainly cost a lot of money. How often do parties look at their structures and meetings and ask how welcoming or appealing they are? There has certainly been a deadening weight of formalities, tradition and bureaucracy in both the CP and the LP. In this aspect, which they share with trade unions in this country, they are more alike than different – perhaps there are more similarities than is usually recognised. The CP was also a broadish church, even if it was not supposed to be, and certainly never set out to be. There was no culture shock in moving to the LP.

Which brings me to my second observation, which concerns the atmosphere in the two parties. I probably delayed joining the LP because of the internecine strife there which mirrored that in the CP. But when I did join the atmosphere was open and relaxed but businesslike. I approved and felt at home and I was welcomed – though perhaps with reservations from a few remaining hard-leftists (I had made no secret of my time in the CP). There were many political differences, but by this time whatever the political differences everyone would still work together. I had a blazing row by e-mail with Hackney's arch-Blairite over Iraq, but when we next met we still worked happily together in an election campaign. Discussions could get heated at the GC, but almost always remained within correct limits. And I was pleased in both Hackney and Kendal to find that conversations and discussions were amicable, and that the old divisions between left and right were not just muted but of surprisingly little significance. The old Labour right wing that we in the CP had demonised simply did not exist locally.

By the time we left Hackney in 2004, our Labour councillors were an elderly Muslim, a middle-aged Jewish liberal and a young white atheist; neighbouring wards had Turkish and young Afro-Caribbean ones: Hackney at its diverse best. We had a good social life, too. In Kendal, where councillors were being removed from power, there was bitterness directed at the Lib-Dems, but it could also become internalised and was occasionally directed at fellow members. There was also a lack of political discussion. Despite this, the members are an impressive collective of great experience and varied skills, and we are now having some high-quality debates. An influx of new members helped, even if they were 'incomers' and took a little time to earn respect! I was delighted to find that one of our new members was the CPGB's last West of England District Secretary. This was different to Hackney, where an extremely high turnover in population was the norm, and comrades came and went with much rapidity.

SUMMARY

I don't regret my years in the CPGB at all. My current life – personal, professional and political – is an extension of those years. I received a political education there which will stay with me throughout my activist life. I cannot deny an emotional attachment to the CP. I read some of the material still being produced about the CP with pleasure and interest. But it's not an obsession and I don't wallow in nostalgia – I hope I look to the future as much as the past. At sixty, I'm more active than ever and happy in my choices – though I do intend to take a partial political sabbatical to attempt to complete two long-standing projects: a book on Britain and the Paris Commune and a printed version of my bibliography of the CPGB. Retirement, political or professional, is not on the agenda.

One can never know what the future holds politically, but I expect that for some years to come I'll be working in the Labour Party and WDM, and active in other campaigns that will inevitably turn up, practising some sort of what I can only call radical reformism – if that phrase is not too pompous or vague – or at least paying my rent, in Alice Walker's memorable phrase.

The democratisation of everything

Andy Croft

My name is Andy and I am a communist. As the AA mantra says, you have to know your condition before you can do anything about it. It is not that political belief is an illness (although many of our political leaders may make us nauseous). But it can certainly become a habit of imagination, a condition of thinking. As Adrian Mitchell used to say, my heart is still on the left. The alcoholic who has not had a drink for twenty years is still an alcoholic. It is twenty years since I held a party card, but I cannot pretend that I am not still a communist. I even have an occasionally recurring dream in which the party still exists. How sad is that? Well, not quite as sad as the realisation that the human dream of economic, political and cultural democracy was defeated in our lifetimes, on our watch. After the unification of Germany, somebody wrote on the monument to Marx and Engels in Berlin, 'we'll do better next time'. The problem is that it doesn't look like there is going to be a next time.

And yet I still cannot believe that there are not better ways of organising society than our present arrangements. After a quarter of a million years on this little planet, we ought to be able to look after ourselves and each other (and the planet) a bit better. There is an early Iain M. Banks science-fiction story in which the Culture – a technologically sophisticated and egalitarian civilisation – visit Earth. The Culture emissaries are appalled to find a humanoid species which has discovered nuclear power and space-travel so quickly, but which is still mired in violent and primitive ideas of religion, empire, class and private property. Their first instinct is to destroy the infection before it spreads:

When they are not actually slaughtering each other they're inventing ingenious new ways to massacre each other in the future, and when they're not doing that they're committing speciescide, from the Amazon to Borneo ... or filling the seas with shit, or the air, or the land ... I wanted to hit the place with a programme Lev Davidovitch would have been proud of. I wanted to see the junta generals fill their pants when they realised that the future is – in Earth terms – bright, bright red.

The twentieth-century communist tradition represented the best attempt so far to make the earth a little bit 'redder'. It also committed the most appalling crimes in trying to do so. We have to know the worst before we can imagine the best. And for anyone on the left, especially the ex-communist or post-communist left, we have to begin by acknowledging our contribution to the worst. To describe yourself as a communist these days sounds like a wilful admission of madness or badness, especially now that, in Europe at least, the equation of communism with fascism is an intellectual commonplace. Anyway, most people under thirty don't know what the word means, beyond a vague idea that it was A Very Bad Thing, involving cold temperatures, walls and barbed wire.

JOINING

I finally joined the Party in 1983, after several years of eager fellow-travelling. In retrospect it was a decision waiting to happen. I was born in 1956 (between the Khrushchev Speech and the invasion of Hungary) in Handforth, Cheshire, now a part of Greater Manchester. My dad was a radio-electronics engineer who worked on the Blue Streak guided missile system, later in computers. My mum worked as a secretary in a local comprehensive school. They read the *Daily Telegraph* and the *Methodist Recorder*. I cannot remember a single political conversation in my childhood (my parents even refused to say how they voted). But I do remember a lot of hostility to the idea of politics. My dad hated trades unions. I remember him growling when Mick McGahey and Hugh Scanlon were on *Any Questions*. He once tore up a copy of *Private Eye* I had left lying around.

The strongest intellectual influence on my childhood was the Methodist chapel to which we were taken every Sunday. My dad played the organ; my mum sang in the choir. By the time I was seventeen I was teaching in Sunday School. Although I left that world behind a very long time ago, my thinking is unavoidably shaped by that part of the Puritan moral vocabulary which requires us to bear witness, to testify on behalf of the speechless against the Pharisees, the powerful, the hypocrites and the liars. When I was a boy, Christ's denunciation of the moneylenders in the temple never failed to excite me. And the Nonconformist churches were miles ahead of the rest of British society in thinking about the Third World, the environment and the politics of under-development. My imagination is still patterned by the Puritan language of English Nonconformity – Manichean, antinomian and millenarian. The blurb on the back of my first book of poems, *Nowhere Special*, described it as being located somewhere 'between pessimism of the intellect and the chiliasm of despair' (or for those who recognised the quotations, between Gramsci and Edward Thompson). And of course all those years of standing in chapel and Sunday School with a hymn book in my hand gave me an over-developed sense of rhythm, rhyme and stanza form, of the power of metrical expectation and of shared symbolic language. The first poem I ever had published – at the age of eleven in the local newspaper – was a solemn little acrostic about the war in Biafra ('B for Biafra where there's bloodshed everywhere / I for the ignorance of people who don't care ...').

I went to the local grammar school, where of course we were given *Animal Farm* to read (the teacher had to tell us about the Russian revolution so we would understand the allegory). Later we were expected to read *Lord of the Flies*. If there was a revolution in the 1960s, nobody told us. English O-level left me completely cold. At the same time, however, we were given some Catullus to translate in Latin. I had never read anything like it. Toxic stuff to give a sixteen-year-old. It was a real revelation, and the point at which I think I knew I wanted to write poetry. Especially when I realised how much my dad hated it.

An English degree taught me a lot about reading poetry, but not much about writing it; even less about the relationship between poetry and politics (I remember a visiting US academic arguing that

Thomas More's *Utopia* was an *anti*-Communist satire). Not that there was much politics at Nottingham University in the late 1970s. In my first week I went to hear Tariq Ali speak at an IMG meeting on the campus. I arrived early, expecting to find an audience of hundreds; of course there were less than a dozen people there. Student politics at Nottingham seemed to be limited to the annual attempt by the Conservatives to persuade the union to leave the NUS. They were not successful. Nor was the campus Maoist who once stood for union president on a promise to close all the union bars. Politics seemed like a joke.

The impact of Thatcher changed all that. By 1979 it was impossible to avoid 'politics'. The great setpiece conflicts of the early Thatcher years – unemployment, cruise missiles, the Falklands War, the miners' strike, South Africa, Nicaragua – naturally appealed to my dualistic imagination. The battle lines could hardly have been clearer. Unfortunately, I made the mistake of joining the Labour Party, then fatally preoccupied with its own internal battles.

I first came across the CP around 1980, while working as a part-time tutor at Nottingham University's adult education centre on Shakespeare Street. There was often a copy of the *Morning Star* to be found there. Compared to the ultra-left sects who somehow managed to be simultaneously ridiculous, unpleasant and dull, and a Labour Party that never actually did anything, the range and seriousness of the CP's political, intellectual and international reach was compelling. I attended public meetings in the city organised by the CP. I ran a half-marathon to raise money for the *Star*. I attended the last Communist University of London. My first book reviews were published in *Labour Monthly* and the *Star*. My second published poem appeared in *Artery*. It was only a matter of time before I joined the party.

The day that the USA invaded Grenada, Dennis Healy and Geoffrey Howe were wheeled onto *The World at One* to justify the invasion as a choice between 'Democracy and Communism'. If Reagan and Thatcher represented Democracy and Maurice Bishop represented Communism, I knew which side I was on. I resigned from the Labour Party and applied to join the CP that day.

I had just moved to Teesside in order to take up a teaching job at

Leeds University's adult education centre in Middlesbrough, teaching and organising evening courses, week-end schools and summer schools in Literature and Creative Writing. It was my first full-time job. I had also just become a dad. New job, new town, new baby, new political party. What could possibly go wrong?

TAKING PART

All the histories of the CP's last years are predicated on an idea of moribund districts, paper branches and rapidly exiting members, as the background to a political drama taking place elsewhere. And yet in its last decade, the party was actually growing in membership and activity on Teesside. The Northern District may have been paralysed for several years by the growing divisions in the party, but the Middlesbrough branch was relatively untouched by these arguments. The small neighbouring Stockton branch was implacably opposed to the direction of the party, but – apart from an annual *Morning Star* bazaar – they never engaged in any public activity. After the internalised political life of the Labour Party, Communist Party meetings were a complete revelation. The first meeting I attended was a discussion of George Orwell and *Nineteen Eighty-four*. The first responsibility I was given was to help organise a money-raising social featuring Sankomota, a band from Lesotho, for the Roads to Freedom sponsored bike-ride.

The Middlesbrough branch of the party was traditionally a large and overwhelmingly working-class branch, with a distinguished record of local campaigns and public agitations, influential in the shipbuilding, steel, railway and local government trade unions. In the 1920s, the Party had led the NUWM in a bitterly fought struggle to hold public meetings at Stockton Cross. In the 1930s, communists led the campaign against the BUF on Teesside. In 1938, the party successfully persuaded Middlesbrough dockers not to load the SS *Haruna Maru* with pig-iron bound for Japan, the first of a series of industrial actions in British ports taken in protest at the Japanese war-effort in Manchuria. A number of Teesside party members fought in Spain, most notably Dave Goodman, Dave Marshall, Tommy Chilvers, Jim Worton and John Longstaff. Tommy Chilvers later engraved the memorial plaque to the Teesside International Brigaders now hanging in Middlesbrough Town Hall.

Prominent local Party members had included George Short, who had trained at the Lenin School in Moscow in the early 1930s; John McDonald, who used a Union Jack as his doormat; the Unity Theatre, RSC and *Coronation Street* actress Anne Dyson; Maurice Sutherland (later Labour chair of Cleveland County Council); the distinguished ICI scientist Norman Levy; the long-standing President of Middlesbrough Trades Council, Jack Feeney; and – according to Brian Clough – the Middlesbrough goalkeeper Peter Taylor. In its last years party members included the writers Bert Ward, John Longden and Nina Hibbin, formerly the film critic of the *Daily Worker* (and *The Lady*).

In the 1930s the YCL had their own premises in Middlesbrough; YCL members started Teesside Unity Theatre, taking political sketches round working men's clubs in the town. For many years the Party had offices on Grange Road. During the Second World War Teesside was strong enough to be organised as a Party District, with George Short as Secretary. After the war, the party was variously involved in the Squatters' Movement, the Peace Movement, the CRE, the Pensioners' Movement and the Trades Council. During the 1966 World Cup, the branch made a presentation to the North Korean team playing their group matches at Ayresome Park.

Although never in a position to seriously challenge the Labour Party machine in elections, the party had a long tradition of standing candidates (in the 1940s the Party won several seats on Stockton Council), if only to ensure that there would be more than one candidate, and therefore an election. Over the years the party had established itself as a lively alternative to the brain-dead combination of careerism, patronage, intellectual inertia and one-more-push electoralism of a Labour Party that had no presence in the life of the town between elections.

While the left in the local Labour Party spent the 1980s trying, without success, to de-select MP Stuart Bell, the CP branch held twice-monthly open meetings, published a monthly newsletter, and ran a popular travelling bookstall. We stood candidates in local elections, went leafleting and fly-posting, ran jumble-sales, sold *7 Days* in the town centre on Saturday mornings, published regular letters in the *Evening Gazette*, and demonstrated against South African goods in supermarkets. There was a small but lively YCL branch, we started a Men's Group and a *Marxism Today* discussion group, and we worked with local churches to organise One World Week. We published a series of historical pamphlets, notably Dave Goodman's Spanish Civil War memoir *From the Tees to the Ebro*, Bert Ward's *I'll See Socialism in My Time* and Arthur Clegg's *From Middlesbrough to Manchuria: the Story of the Haruna Maru*. A young comrade at the local art college designed and made a new branch banner; we even had our own T-shirts printed.

We were responsible for organising the Middlesbrough-York legs of the Big Red Bike Ride, and hosted a series of big money-raising solidarity concerts – for the ANC, Nicaragua Solidarity, Chile Solidarity, CODIR, CADRI, Anti-Apartheid and CND. We ran a programme of education meetings on Marxist theory, and held public meetings with local, national and international on issues of the moment – for example on the miners' strike, Iraq, Iran, Section 28, children's television, Palestine, William Morris, Nicaragua, the Poll Tax, South Africa and the 1987 Abortion (Amendment) bill. Gordon McLennan spoke at a big public meeting shortly after he met with Mikhail Gorbachev. We held debates with the ILP and with the SWP. Martin Jacques came up to debate with the leader of Middlesbrough Council, Mike Carr. In 1989 we organised 'What's Left?' – a two day conference of seminars and debates with speakers from local trades union and community groups. Cleveland against the War in the Gulf was established at an open meeting called by the branch.

The branch's last significant intervention in local – and briefly, national – life, was during the 1987 Cleveland Child Abuse crisis. We called a meeting, at which over two hundred people heard Bea Campbell begin to develop the analysis that would later be published as *Unofficial Secrets*. At that meeting a decision was taken to establish the Cleveland Campaign against the Sexual Abuse of Children (CAUSE). For our efforts, we were denounced by Stuart Bell in a double-page article in the *Daily Mail*, warning darkly of a 'Communist-Lesbian plot' to overthrow the family.

In 1989, Teesside communists were involved in establishing Writearound, an annual Cleveland-wide community-writing festival. One of the branch's last acts was to organise an open poetry-reading in protest at the invasion of Iraq. When the party was dissolved, the book-stall account was used to set up Mudfog Press, a small poetry press still publishing local writers.

BEING A PART

In short, this was a busy, friendly, active organisation, a space where people could pool their energies, share their concerns and collectively develop their responses through open discussion and inclusive activity. The party was always a great place for an argument, for principled, reasoned disagreements. I loved it. All of it. There was no task too menial or too boring that I would not undertake for the party. I worked very hard for the organisation, as membership secretary, literature secretary, branch secretary, area committee member, district committee member and eventually as the last Northern District secretary – organising meetings, booking rooms, writing newsletters, booking bands, obtaining drinks licenses, stuffing envelopes, leafleting and flyposting, delivering a weekly *7 Days* round, collecting speakers from Darlington station, speaking, chairing meetings, writing minutes, typing agendas, putting the chairs out. But the party gave me back much more – it gave my life purpose and meaning, shaping my political imagination, expectations and reflexes. It brought me into contact with a great many extraordinary and selfless people, from whom I learned a great deal. And I miss it. All of it – the activity, the comradeship, the sense of inhabiting a shared historical narrative, of belonging to an organisation that was always much bigger than the sum of its parts. The party's historical international loyalties may often have been an unsupportable burden, but as late as the 1980s they were also a continuing source of pride (the SACP, the PCI, Gorbachev).

Teaching in university adult education always felt like a perfect fit for a communist (Edward Thompson had taught literature for Leeds University's adult education department after the war), discussing books and ideas with working-class adults, helping to develop a native Teesside literary scene. Through the party I came to know a number of distinguished writers, particularly Margot Heinemann, Jack Lindsay and Arnold Rattenbury, who were each extremely encouraging of my first efforts at writing poetry and criticism. Between them, they tried to teach me how to write. By the mid-1980s I was writing for *7 Days, Marxism Today* and *Red Letters*. My first book, *Red Letter Days* – a study of British Popular Front fiction – was of course published by Lawrence and Wishart. I wrote and presented a series of programmes about mostly CP writers from the 1930s, based on the book, for Radio Four.

I suppose my position would have been described as a 'centrist'. My overwhelming loyalty was to the party and its activities, not to any of its competing factions or tendencies. I supported the leadership of Gordon McLennan and Nina Temple, but if the 'opposition' had won control I would probably have remained in the party. At the same time, it was clear that the Party's developing analysis, as it emerged through the pages of *Marxism Today*, then in *Manifesto for New Times*, was irresistibly compelling. The implications may have been hard to swallow, but it was the only serious account to make sense of the rapid changes taking place in Thatcherite Britain. Long after the other institutions on the British left had fossilised into cartoon versions of themselves, the party was still taking intellectual risks. One of the attractive things about the party was the sudden access of humility it enjoyed in its last years. While it was apparent to everyone that we no longer knew the answers, we were still interested in asking questions.

Moreover, the Gramscian analysis of the changing balance of political, social and cultural forces, seemed to me to be wholly consistent with the development of the party's positions since the middle 1930s. From the United Front, the Popular Front and the anti-Fascist war, via *The British Road to Socialism* and the Alternative Economic Strategy to *MT* and New Times, the party was most effective when it sought the democratic mobilisation of the greatest number of people around winnable positions. An organisation with such a weak purchase on British life always needed allies. It had enough enemies already.

ENDING

At first I was horrified by the EC's proposals to transform the party into what became Democratic Left. I could have been persuaded to oppose the EC's proposals if the opposition had not been so unremittingly committed to defending the indefensible aspects of the communist tradition. After a lot of hard thinking, I was persuaded that ending the party was the best way of saving it. At the time it seemed the last chance we had to rescue something from the wreckage, to escape from the overwhelming burden of the party's bad memories. By 1991 the European communist tradition had become untenable. If the PCI thought the game was up, who was I to argue? It also seemed like an opportunity to build on the experiences of the party on Teesside, where we had been successful to the extent that we were able to involve people who were not members of any political party. I even spoke at the last Congress to our branch's amendment proposing the removal of the word 'party' from the draft constitution of Democratic Left.

It should have been a liberation. It was a disaster. Most party members on Teesside did not join the new organisation, including those who had supported it in the pre-Congress discussions. Overnight a busy and energetic organisation was reduced to a handful of confused individuals. When, at our first meeting, we discussed the election of branch officers in order to get things done, a visiting EC member admonished us for still being locked into 'old politics'. So we did nothing. DL asked nothing of me, and I gave it nothing back. I stayed out of loyalty to a bad decision until the transformation to the New Times Network in 1998 gave me the opportunity to slip away quietly, still ashamed to have been complicit in exchanging something valuable for something so useless and so risible.

I still live with an overwhelming sense of loss. The end of the party was the first of a series of abrupt endings which have shaped my life with disappointment and dismay. About the same time as the party was dissolved, my first marriage broke up. Not long afterwards, Leeds University closed its adult education centre in Middlesbrough; the building was sold, knocked down and replaced by flats. I resigned from Leeds University, which, like most British universities, is no longer interested in teaching working-class adults. A new editor passing through the *Evening Gazette* closed down my weekly poetry column in the paper. The Writearound festival folded after eleven years. In the name of 'Producer Choice', my Radio Four producer lost his job and I lost my access to programme making. One of the last programmes we made together was a thirty-minute documentary about the end of the party and its literary traditions. Suddenly I was a poet without a living tradition, an adult educator without a classroom, a part-time dad, a communist without a party.

WRITING

I was thirty-five when the party finally unravelled itself. Now I am fifty-five. The last two decades have been years of great personal happiness, in which Nikki and I have brought up our children together and sent them out into the world. Since 1991 I have published a great many books and given poetry-readings all over the UK; last year I read in Moscow, New York and Siberia. This should be enough. And so it is. But I can't pretend that I don't still feel a kind of nagging intellectual agoraphobia. The desert horizon is limitless, but I don't know in which direction to walk. So I walk backwards.

Every election I end up writing 'none of the above' on the ballot paper. I am still a member of CND, I was involved in the Yes campaign during the referendum for a Northern Assembly, and I am still on the editorial board of *Socialist History*. After a break of twenty years, I started reading the *Morning Star* again. I disagree with the paper's hostility to the EU, and cannot take seriously its belief in the prospect of reclaiming the Labour Party. But it is a lot more readable, a lot less sectarian than it used to be. For the last nine years I have written a regular monthly poetry column for the paper.

In a sense, all my writing since 1991 has been an attempt to stop the sand blowing over the ruins until a younger generation can rediscover the necessity of democratic revolutionary change, by trying to keep books in print and writers in circulation. Specifically, books like *Red Letter Days, Out of the Old Earth, Comrade Heart, A Weapon in the Struggle, Selected Poems of Randall Swingler* and *Red Sky at Night* (edited with Adrian Mitchell) sought to rescue aspects of the party's remarkably rich literary history from the usual lazy cold-war caricatures of Russophilia and clenched fisted propaganda. No political organisation ever took imaginative writing so seriously, or contributed so much to British cultural life as the CP once did. Most histories of the party attend rather more carefully to the party's relationship with the Soviet Union, to its industrial struggles and its anti-colonial and peace campaigns than to its cultural life. And yet the party's literary culture may prove to be one of its most enduring achievements. For over seventy years the British Communist Party conducted a sustained imaginative intervention in British literary life, quite out of proportion to either its size or political influence. In European terms, none of this may seem remarkable. But in the context of British political life it is a unique and extraordinary record. British political culture is generally afraid of the arts, as British artistic culture is hostile to politics. Economism and electoralism leave little room for the imagination. The party represented a long-term, educational project to debate and popularise ideas about the relationship between understanding and action, between culture and politics, writers and readers, literature and society. British life has hardly been improved by its disappearance, or by the ruthless airbrushing of the party's literary achievements from the historical record.

I set up Smokestack Books in 2004, partly as an attempt to promote the work of radical poets whose work has been unavailable in Britain – Nikola Vaptsarov (Bulgaria), Francis Combes (France), Martín Espada (Puerto Rico), Victor Jara (Chile), Andras Mezei (Hungary), Gustavo Pereira (Venezuela) and Jim Scully (USA). One of Smokestack's earliest titles was the *Collected Poems of Tom Wintringham*, the first commander of the British Battalion in Spain. One of Smokestack's most recent titles was *A Rose Loupt Oot: Poetry and Song Celebrating the UCS Work-in*.

Writing sometimes feels like a poor substitute for participating in civil society. Nevertheless, writing, especially poetry, allows me to say things that I cannot say in other ways. The other things I do – working in schools and prisons, writing books for children – are simply ways of extending the conversation. Several collections of poetry, notably *Nowhere Special, Just as Blue, Comrade Laughter* and *Sticky*, have tried in their different ways to describe the long defeat of Utopianism that began in 1991. Two comic-novels in verse, *Ghost Writer* and *Nineteen Forty-eight*, have proposed counter-factual narratives to aspects of communist history. *Three Men on the Metro* (written with Bill Herbert and Paul Summers) explicitly addressed elements of Soviet history, its utopianism and its cynicism, its heroism and its crimes, its victories and its defeats.

I don't write about 'politics', certainly not about political parties, government legislation or parliamentary elections. But I am interested in the relationship between the powerful and the powerless, in the uses and abuses of power, and the ways in which the powerful maintain their positions and privileges. You do not have to be interested in politics to be repulsed by ludicrous and violent figures like Blair, Sarkozy, Bush, Berlusconi, Putin and Cameron. My definition of 'politics' in this sense would be something like St Paul's – 'For we do not wrestle only against flesh and blood, but against principalities, against powers, against the rulers of the darkness of this age, against spiritual hosts of wickedness in the heavenly places.'

The great communist poets of the twentieth-century – Ritsos, Aragon, Neruda, Hikmet, Vaptsarov, Alberti, Éluard, Hernandez, Vallejo, Brecht – lived in a period of rapid social and political change. They grew up in the newly-literate, urbanising societies of the early twentieth century, characterised by new mass media, mass politics and mass participation in civil society. Their writings were shaped first by their involvement in the early Modernist movements, and then by their rejection of Modernism, articulating more democratic ways of responding to the challenges of Modernity. Between them they lived through war, revolution, economic depression, fascism, civil war, illegality, prison and exile. These were the circumstances out of which they created the most extraordinary body of work. While they may seem unlikely ingredients in the creation of exceptional poetry, we can see now that it was these exceptional conditions that made them.

These poets made poetry out of politics and took politics into the worlds of poetry. They were able to write about the private and the public, the lyrical and the satirical, the utopian and the historical, combining documentary record, formal experimental and traditional forms. They were all great love poets. They each celebrated the poetry of everyday life, of everyday objects – as Ritsos called it, 'the celestial side by side / with the everyday'. And they insisted on the poetry of ordinary language, demotic, colloquial speech. Above all, they found ways of synthesising the struggles for personal, political and national liberation as a single narrative – consider the poetry which Hikmet wrote in Istanbul and Bursa prisons, Brecht's 'Svendborg Poems', Neruda's *Canto General*, Aragon's *Le Crève-Coeur*, Vaptsarov's *Motor Songs*, or Ritsos's *Romiossini*.

The political circumstances today are wholly different. But the questions these writers tried to answer to still need to be asked, in our own time. We too need a new relationship between the intelligentsia and society, between writers and readers, between poetry and politics. Poetry is uniquely placed to familiarise, popularise and mobilise ideas and feelings. It can combine memorable performance and quiet reflection, immediacy and enjoyment. And it can express a shared common sense counter to the prevailing narratives of government and national media. Poetry is still, potentially, a way of saying things that cannot be said in other ways; a place of refusal and dissent, of public testimony and personal affirmation, of generous vision and imagination.

Unfortunately poetry and politics in Britain are expected to occupy separate, if not antagonistic worlds, as with notions of the private and the public. Demotic language is now the poetry of advertising; British society is inoculated against the music of poetry just as much as it is against socialist or democratic ideas. British mainstream culture is very good at recognising what it already knows. Although it talks a lot about the 'new', the Next Big Thing usually turns out to be just like last year's dull model. Poets, readers and publishers are increasingly squeezed between Arts Council cuts, high-street monopolies, internet price-wars, Creative Writing battery-farms and book-signing festivals. Just as the democratic process is increasingly blocked by political inertia, authoritarianism and deceit, the contemporary poetry scene chokes on self-promotion, celebrity prizes and the travelling festival circus.

Hugo Williams, prize-winning poet and a Forward Prize judge, recently complained that these days there are too many entries to the competition: 'I think it's something to do with the democratisation of everything – that everyone's got a right to get a book out. I've got the feeling that sometimes it's more about desire than worth ...' In a sense he was right. Poetry *is* about the 'democratisation of everything'. It's a way of extending the common ownership of experience, feeling and language. Poetry is a Republic, not a meritocracy of the lucky, the talented or the privately educated. It requires the proper democratic humility necessary for any art. That's why it scares old Etonian cultural gate-keepers like Hugo Williams. And why contemporary British poetry, like the body politic, is dying on its feet.

BEING APART

'Communism' was, for me, always about the 'democratisation of everything'. It was defeated in the name of Democracy, and now politics is again the preserve of a tiny, wealthy elite. The public's only role is to legitimise their depredations by swelling the crowd-scenes for the tv cameras every five years. At best we are spectators to a series of palace revolutions (Blair-Brown, MPs' expenses, the banking crises, News International). At suitable intervals minor players are thrown to the crowd in a parody of democratic process. But it is no longer anything to do with us.

At the time of writing, Britain is at war again for the fifth time in twenty years. The dishonest pretexts for each new round of imperial slaughter become increasingly implausible. The narrow, consensual space between Cameron, Clegg and Miliband means that the only permissible debate regarding the continued military occupation of Afghanistan appears to be about helicopters and body-armour; public discussion of the riots of 2011 was quickly boiled down to racist dog-whistles about law and order, national service and capital punishment. Anyone who thinks that a New Labour revival is the answer has forgotten what the question was.

There is no point underestimating the seriousness of the situation. We still don't understand the extent to which progressive ideas and forces have been defeated, at least in Europe, in the last twenty years. The victory march of the right – economic libertarians, social authoritarians and violent imperialists – has been accompanied by the atrophying of the political process and the narrowing of democratic discourse. There is not much room for internationalism between the ugly nationalisms of the far right, the brutal supra-nationalism of the EU and the violent internationalism of globalisation. From the current European-wide assault on the welfare infrastructure to air strikes in Libya, there is no alternative narrative to the triumphal history of the victors.

It would be foolish to argue that anything could have been different if the party had survived the fall of Gorbachev. In retrospect, it seems incredible that the party lasted as long as it did. The space it once occupied – combining local activity and international solidarity, intellectual enquiry and cultural innovation, philosophical analysis and day-to-day campaigning – has long since closed down. But as a result, I live apart from the society in which I find myself, and not as a part of it. The Communist Party, for all its comic-opera absurdity, its spectacular hubris and its self-defeating innocence, was a congenial and habitable political space that offered a way of participating in and of belonging to the world. I want it back.

Notes on contributors

Dave Cope runs Britain's largest radical second-hand book business, Left on the Shelf.

Andy Croft is a poet, publisher and children's writer.

Alistair Findlay is a former professional footballer and a recently retired social-worker. He is a poet.

Stuart Hill is a Labour councillor in North Tyneside.

Kate Hudson is General Secretary of CND.

Andrew Pearmain is a research fellow at UEA, and a consultant practitioner in HIV/AIDS social care.

Mark Perryman is the co-founder of the self-styled 'sporting outfitters of intellectual distinction', Philosophy Football.

Lorna Reith is deputy leader of Haringey Council and cabinet member for Children.

Select Index

Aaronovitch, David 74-6
Aaronovitch, Sam 13
Abbott, Diane 129
African National Congress/ANC 144
Airlie, Jimmy 66
Alberti, Rafael 150
Ali, Tariq 14, 141
Almond, Gabriel 9
Anti-Apartheid Movement 8, 144
Anti-Nazi League 11
Archer, Robyn 78
Aragon, Louis 150
Artery 141
Ashton, Jack 111
Aswad 12
Atkinson, Eric 52

Banks, Ian M. 138
Baudrillard, Jean 25
Beat the Blues Festival 15
Bell, Stuart 143
Bernal, J.D. 8
Beyond the Fragments 12
Bishop, Maurice 141
Bisky, Lothar 42
Blair, Tony 22-3, 30, 55, 99
Brecht, Bert 7, 10, 57, 80
British Road to Socialism, The 19, 53, 61, 70, 71, 78, 93, 125, 146

British Soviet Friendship Society 122
Brown, Gordon 24, 55, 99
Bukharin, Nikolai 42
Burns, Robert 52

Cable Street 8
CADRI (Committee against Repression and for Democratic Rights in Iraq) 144
Calder, Angus 57, 65
Campaign for a Scottish Assembly 55, 61
Campbell, Beatrix 8, 15, 52, 110
Canavan, Dennis 56
Carrillo, Santiago 42
Carr, Mike 106, 144
Carter, Pete 111
Catullus 140
Cencrastus 57
Central Books 122-3
Charter 77 94
Charter 88 115
Chater, Tony 126
Chile Solidarity Campaign 8, 91, 92, 94-5, 144
Chilvers, Tommy 142
Clash, The 11
Clegg, Arthur 144
CND (Campaign for Nuclear Disarmament) 8, 16, 43-6, 92, 144, 148

CODIR (Committee for the Defence of the Iranian People's Rights) 144
Collets 79
Combes, Francis 149
Comment 79
Communist Manifesto, The 19, 34, 45, 50
Communist Party of Britain (CPB) 126
Cook, Dave 110
Costello, Elvis 11
Cross, Stefan 112, 114
Cuba Solidarity 26, 108
CUL (Communist University of London) 13, 28, 70, 125

Daily Worker 7, 91, 143
Davis, Angela 108
de Groot, Joanna 111
Democratic Left 7, 29, 96-7, 115, 122, 123, 126, 128, 145-7
Derrida, Jacques 49-51
Die Linke (Germany) 32, 42
Dix, Bernard 106
Duffy, Carol Ann 60
Dyson, Anne 143

Eluard, Paul 150
Espada, Martín 149

Fairley, John 56
Falber, Reuben 108
Feeney, Jack 143
Fielding, Helen 21
Fisher, Alan 106
Flying Pickets, The 79
Foot, Michael 53
Foot, Paul 14

Foster, John 52, 64
Fukuyama, Francis 37, 49

Gallacher, Willie 58, 59, 60
Galloway, George 30
Gaughan, Dick 53, 54
General Strike, 1926 8
Gibson, John 122
Given, Quentin 89
GMB 105, 111-3
Gold, Harry 35
Goodenough, Eileen 112
Goodman, Dave 142, 144
Gorbachev, Mikhail 144, 145, 152
Gove, Michael 21
Gramsci, Antonio 13, 14, 19, 24, 27, 42, 58, 71, 83, 140
Gray, Alasdair 64
Grossman, Vasily 83
Guevara, Che 35

Hall, Stuart 13, 27, 52
Hambling, Maggie 65
Harland, Andrew 105
Heinemann, Margot 145
Henderson, Hamish 8, 58, 61
Herbert, Bill 149
Hernandez, Miguel 150
Hibbin, Nina 143
Hill, Joe 48
Ho Chi Min 96
Hobsbawm, Eric 13, 27

ILP (Independent Labour Party) 144
IMG (International Marxist Group) 12, 36, 141
International Brigades 8, 143
Izquierda Unida (Spain) 42

Index

Jacques, Martin 19, 144
Jones, Claudia 7
Jones, Ernie 104

Kautsky, Karl 45
Kay, Jack 121
Kay, John 54
King, Oona 30

Labour Monthly 34, 141
Lady, The 143
Lawrence and Wishart 122, 146
Lenin, Vladimir 45, 58, 124, 129
Leonard, Tom 60
Lessing, Doris 7
Leveller, The 12
Levy, Martin 105
Levy, Norman 143
Liebknecht, Karl 42
Lindsay, Jack 145
Livingstone, Ken 30, 31, 128
Lochhead, Liz 60
Loftus, Maria 111
Longden, John 143
Longstaff, John 142
Luxemburg, Rosa 42

MacDiarmid, Hugh 7, 57, 58, 60
McDonald, John 143
McGahey, Mick 8, 13, 52, 54, 65-66, 139
McKay, Ian 111
MacLean, John 58
McLennan, Gordon 54, 126, 144, 146
Make Poverty History Campaign 132
Mandelson, Peter 55
Manifesto for New Times 20, 146

Marshall, Dave 142
Marx Memorial Library 126
Marx, Karl 38, 39, 49, 51
Marxism Today 8, 13, 14, 16, 17-25, 27, 54, 55, 56, 57, 78, 125, 127, 144, 146
Medical Aid for Vietnam 91, 103
Mezei, Andras 149
Milburn, Alan 116
Miliband, Ed 24, 99
Militant Tendency 31, 55
Mitchell, Adrian 148
Moore, Henry 7
Moore, Thomas 141
Morgan, Edwin 60
Morning Star 8, 16, 35, 54, 55, 63, 64, 77, 79, 91, 104, 123, 126 141, 142, 148
Morris, William 144
Movement for Colonial Freedom 8

Nairn, Tom 61
NALGO (National Association of Local Government Officers) 52
National Front 11
Neruda, Pablo 57, 150
New Communist Party 126
New Politics Network 115
New Socialist 14, 28
New Times 128
New Times Network 115
Nicaragua Solidarity Campaign 144
Norris, Bill 122
Notting Hill Carnival 8
NUPE (National Union of Public Employees) 105-7, 109, 111
NUS (National Union of Students) 71-7

Orwell, George 8, 49, 140, 142
Osundare, Niyi 57

Paine, Tom 102
Palestine Solidarity Campaign 108, 134
Palme Dutt, Raji 34
Pankhurst, Sylvia 7
Parkinson, Frank 119
Partei des Demokratischen Sozialismus/PDS (Germany) 42
Parti Communiste Français/PCF (France) 42
Partido Comunista de España/PCE (Spain) 42
Partito Comunista Italiano/PCI (Italy) 32, 41, 96, 145, 147
Partito della Rifondazione Comunista (Italy) 32, 42
Pelling, Henry 9
People's Jubilee 89
People's March for Jobs 74
Pereira, Gustavo 149
Philosophy Football 25-8
Piratin, Phil 30
Progressive Books 120
Pursey, Jimmy 11

Radical Scotland 56-7
Ramelson, Bert 67, 109
Rattenbury, Arnold 145
Red Letters 146
Reid, Jimmy 7, 52, 66
Respect 31, 43
Ritsos, Giannis 150
Robinson, Tom 11
Rock Against Racism 11
Rodell Properties 115
Rosselson, Leon 134

Salmond, Alex 62, 63
Scanlon, Hugh 139
Scargill, Arthur 54
Scully, Jim 149
Seven Days 54, 143, 145
Shankly, Bill 25
Shelley, Percy 52
Sheridan, Tommy 62
Shinwell, Manny 33
Short, George 104, 143
Simon, Brian 72
Slits, The 15
Smith, Jim 104
Socialist Action 31
Socialist History 148
Socialist History Society 126
SSP (Scottish Socialist Party) 30, 31, 62
Steel Pulse 11
Stiff Little Fingers 11
Stop the War Coalition (STWC) 46-7
Straight Left 121
Summers, Paul 149
Sutherland, Maurice 143
Swann, Irene 111
Swingler, Randall 148
Swinton, Tilda 7
SWP (Socialist Workers Party) 11, 12, 31, 36, 89, 144

T&G (Transport and General Workers Union) 103, 105, 111
TASS (Technical Administrative and Supervisory Staffs) 103
Taylor, Peter 143
Temple, Nina 79, 111, 146
Thatcher, Margaret 13, 53, 62, 141

Thompson, Edward 7, 27, 140, 145
Thompson, Willie 56
Townsend Warner, Sylvia 8
Tressell, Robert 120-1, 134
Trotsky, Leon 39, 42

UNISON 108, 112-4
United Left Party (Ireland) 32
Unlock Democracy 29, 115
Upper Clyde Shipbuilders 8, 149

Vallejo, César 150
Vaptsarov, Nikola 149, 150
Vietnam Solidarity Campaign 8, 104

Ward, Bert 143
Wedlake, Dave 105

Wesker, Arnold 7
Williams, Hugo 150
Wilson, Elizabeth 52
Wilson, Theodora Wilson 134
Wintringham, Tom 149
Wise, Audrey 14
Wood, Neal 9
Working Class Movement Library 126
World Development Movement 131-2
World Youth Festival 108
Worton, Jim 142
Writearound Festival 144, 147

Yaqoob, Salma 31
YCL (Young Communist League) 34, 104-5, 143, 144